AFRO-AMERICANS '76

BLACK AMERICANS IN THE FOUNDING OF OUR NATION

Written and illustrated by Eugene Winslow

Afro-Am Publishing Co., Inc., Chicago

To Kenneth, who was the catalyst for this work.

Hard Cover ISBN 910030-20-0

Soft Cover ISBN 910030-21-9

Library of Congress Catalog Card Number 75-23936

Manufactured in the United States of America

Table of Contents

III FOUNDING AND GROWTH OF THE NATION

PREFACE

In the pages of our history books, the role of the Afro-American in the founding of our nation has been largely overlooked in favor of the more dramatic political and military achievements of the Euro-Americans. With the celebration of our nation's 200th birthday, this omission becomes damaging distortion.

It is hoped that by providing attractively illustrated, easy-to-read information on the contribution of our largest racial minority, this publication may enrich the observations of our Bicentennial, and help the many patriotic celebrations to reflect that multi-ethnicity which is uniquely American.

For ease of comprehension and variety of utilization, the information is concisely presented in three sections and on three levels. The three sections—Exploration, Revolution, and Founding—are intended to show that the creation of the United States of America began long before and continued years after July 4, 1776. The three levels—Period, Events, and People—are intended to give alternate views of the heritage which is our early history.

The Period section is a concise overview for comparative study by students of history; the Events listing offers dates and information for easy integration into United States History courses; the People section presents illustrated biographies for enlivening supplementary reading.

These alternate views offer potential enrichment not only to our Bicentennial but also to traditional data:

By adding to the predominantly white fabric of our history those many black threads which have both strained and strengthened our mantle of democracy;

By expanding the scope of our knowledge to include a few of the many undercurrent events that influenced, and in some cases guided, the direction and destiny of our nation;

By tangibly and graphically giving recognition to the individual contributions and minority-group achievements that can make our government truly of, by, and for *all* of the people.

The most important thing that is hoped will result from this publication is that those who read it—of whatever age or ethnic origin—will be enlightened, inspired, and motivated to make the dream that was born in Philadelphia some 200 years ago a reality in every city and state, now and in the years to come.

EUGENE WINSLOW

CHICAGO, ILLINOIS
SEPTEMBER, 1975

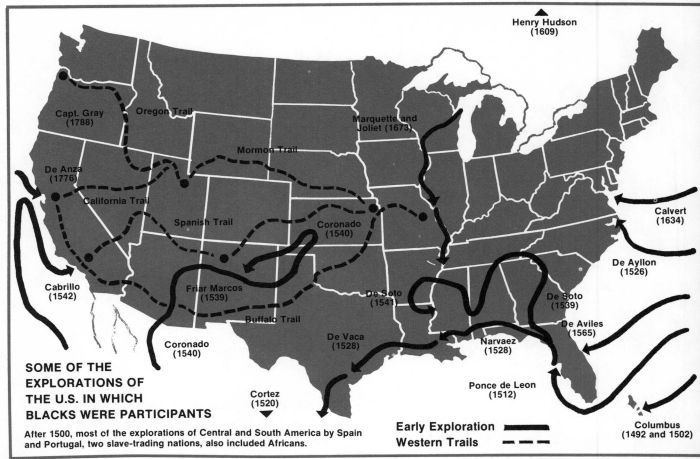

Henry Hudson
(1609)

Capt. Gray
(1788)

Oregon Trail

Marquette and
Joliet (1673)

Mormon Trail

De Anza
(1776)

California Trail

Spanish Trail

Coronado
(1540)

Calvert
(1634)

De Ayllon
(1526)

Cabrillo
(1542)

Friar Marcos
(1539)

De Soto
(1541)

De Soto
(1539)

Buffalo Trail

De Aviles
(1565)

Coronado
(1540)

De Vaca
(1528)

Narvaez
(1528)

Ponce de Leon
(1512)

SOME OF THE
EXPLORATIONS OF
THE U.S. IN WHICH
BLACKS WERE PARTICIPANTS

Cortez
(1520)

Columbus
(1492 and 1502)

After 1500, most of the explorations of Central and South America by Spain
and Portugal, two slave-trading nations, also included Africans.

Early Exploration ▬▬▬▬
Western Trails ▬ ▬ ▬

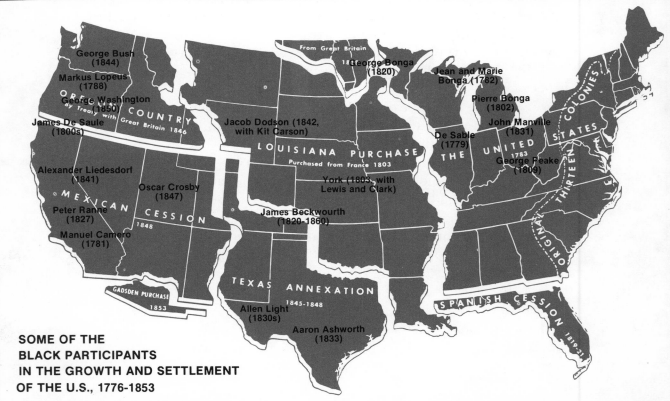

George Bush
(1844)

From Great Britain

George Bonga
(1820)

Jean and Marie
Bonga (1782)

Markus Lopeus
(1788)

ORE

George Washington
(1850)
by Treaty with
Great Britain 1846

COUNTRY

Pierre Bonga
(1802)

James De Saule
(1800s)

Jacob Dodson (1842,
with Kit Carson)

LOUISIANA PURCHASE
Purchased from France 1803

De Sable
(1779)

John Manville
(1831)

THE UNITED STATES

Alexander Liedesdorf
(1841)

MEXICAN

Oscar Crosby
(1847)

York (1803, with
Lewis and Clark)

George Peake
(1809)

ORIGINAL THIRTEEN COLONIES

Peter Ranne
(1827)

CESSION
1848

James Beckwourth
(1820-1860)

Manuel Camero
(1781)

GADSDEN PURCHASE
1853

TEXAS ANNEXATION
1845-1848

SPANISH CESSION
1819-21

Allen Light
(1830s)

Aaron Ashworth
(1833)

SOME OF THE
BLACK PARTICIPANTS
IN THE GROWTH AND SETTLEMENT
OF THE U.S., 1776-1853

The above names are only a few of the hundreds that can be documented. For each that appears in a historical document, there were, of course, thousands of blacks whose presence and participation are not a matter of record. There were black settlers, merchants, miners, and cowboys as well as the slaves who made up a large percentage of the labor force of the period.

I EXPLORATION

AND COLONIZATION OF AMERICA

THE PERIOD: 1440-1775

Just as a human life begins at that moment of conception occuring months before the actual day of birth, our United States of America began in events occuring many, many years before the Declaration of Independence on July 4, 1776, the date accepted as our nation's birthday.

The multi-ethnic "discovery" of America

The rich land we now call America has, of course, existed as long as other parts of the world. A widely held theory is that the true "discoverers" of this land were Mongol tribesmen who arrived here from four to five thousand years before the birth of Christ. Migrating across the Bering Straits when the tides were low, they settled first in the Northwest to become the ancestors of the "Indians" inhabiting the land when the first Europeans arrived.

Records also indicate that the Japanese, the Phoenicians, the Romans and the Chinese all touched upon parts of North and South America hundreds of years before the Norseman, Lief Ericson, who is believed to have landed around what is now Cape Cod, Massachusetts about 1000 A.D.

Christopher Columbus, an Italian-Portuguese sailing under the Spanish flag, landed on one of the Bahama Islands on October 12, 1492. We celebrate this day even though it was not until 1497 that a European set foot on the mainland of America. That year, John Cabot, an Italian sailing under the English flag, explored the coast of Labrador around what is now Newfoundland, Canada. It was in 1513 when the Spaniard, Ponce de Leon, explored Florida that the first European touched upon land that is now considered the United States of America.

The noted black historian Carter G. Woodson was among the first to publicize in the 1920s the belief and evidence that Africans had reached the shores of the "New World" before the Europeans. In the early 1500s, Balboa came upon a race of black men in South America who scholars of the day theorized must have come from the West Coast of Africa thousands of years before. Skulls found in caves in the Bahamas were very similar to those found in the early burial places of the Canaries, an island off the

Some historians believe the pilot on the first voyage of Columbus was an African.

coast of Africa. And Leo Wiener, a Harvard professor, saw evidence of African influence in the life, customs and language of early American Indians.

The Africans as explorers of America

After Africa was "opened up" by European traders in the late 1400s and early 1500s, many natives accompanied the Spanish and Portuguese expeditions to the New World. They came as seamen, soldiers, laborers, servants and slaves. In varying numbers, they accompanied expeditions to Guatemala, Chile, Peru, and Venezuela; were with Columbus, Ponce de Leon, Cabeza de Vaca, Coronado, and De Soto; and played important parts in the exploration of the Florida peninsula, the Mississippi Valley, and the Southwest territories. An African with Cortez in Mexico introduced wheat to the New World when, drawing upon his farming heritage, he planted some grains as an experiment.

While blacks helped construct "the oldest city in the U.S.", St. Augustine, Florida, there may be grounds for their claiming to be the oldest permanent settlers in the U.S.—other than the native Americans, the Indians. The Africans who accompanied Lucas de Ayllón to the Carolinas in 1526 revolted and fled to the forest. When the Spaniards returned to their base in Haiti, the blacks remained behind, possibly establishing a colony pre-dating St. Augustine by more than thirty years; Jamestown, Virginia by almost eighty years; and the Pilgrim's landing at Plymouth Rock by nearly a century.

Many Africans served as seamen and soldiers with the Spanish and Portuguese explorers as early as the fifteenth century.

Sketch from a painting by Grosbeck of Cabrillo landing at Santa Barbara in 1542.

The Africans as colonists

Traditional history has created two wrong impressions about the Afro-Americans of the colonial period: first, that all blacks who came to America were enslaved immediately upon debarkation and remained slaves all their lives; and second, that because most blacks were slaves they therefore were not colonists. However, dictionaries define a colonist as "an original settler of a colony, or an inhabitant of a colony"; there is no qualifying criteria as to status or race. Among the first settlers of the thirteen original colonies were hundreds of indentured servants, black and white; and in the South, many colonies soon had more black inhabitants than white. As the primary labor force of the colonies, these servants and slaves made contributions as crucial to the success of the early settlements as were made by the colonial landowners, merchants, or government officials.

Slave-Colonists. Slavery was unknown to English law, and the first Africans—"Twenty negars"—to arrive in Jamestown in 1619 were sold as indentured servants eligible for freedom after a certain number of years. Slavery was instituted by the settlers when they began making exceptions in the case of black indentured servants—requiring that they serve for life—because whites and Indians did not meet the labor needs of the colonies.

As slaves, the Africans were indispensable in raising the tobacco of Virginia, North Carolina and Maryland; and the rice and indigo of South Carolina. But not all Southern slaves worked in the fields. Some were servants, guards, boatmen or river pilots, and others became skilled craftsmen and builders such as those who built the mansions of Mount Vernon and Monticello. Although less numerous in the New England colonies, slaves took part in every

Africans gradually replaced Europeans and Indians as slave laborers in the North as well as the South.

phase of the diverse economic life of the North. It is recorded that twenty-four slave women worked in a Rhode Island creamery; black craftsmen helped build the Touro Synagogue in Newport; and a New Hampshire paper had a slave pressman. In 1729, a slave obtained his freedom for revealing an herb by which "wonderful cures had been affected".

They also helped clear the forests, drain the swamps, plow the fields, and cultivate the life-giving crops. Some were used to build roads and man the ships, while others were trained to be carpenters, blacksmiths, goldsmiths, silversmiths, sailmakers shipbuilders, and tanners. As laborer or artisan, these slaves were inextricably involved in the settlement of America, and few deny the value of black contributions to early progress.

West Ford, a slave at Mount Vernon, was a skilled artisan, plow-maker and repairer.

Gustavus Vassa, born in Africa in 1745, was kidnapped from Africa at the age of eleven, but bought his freedom from his Quaker owner in 1773 before going to England to live in 1777.

The majority of the slaves, particularly in the South, were cruelly treated; and many, even in the North, sought to change their status. As early as the mid-1600s slaves began conspiring to rebel, and in the following decades revolts broke out in several of the colonies, north and south. In 1770, there were almost 700,000 slaves in the thirteen colonies: 3,763 in New England; 36,323 in the Middle Colonies; and 656,538 in the South. By the time the Revolutionary War began, the slave population exceeded the white population in many areas of the south, and the question of slavery and the problems surrounding the owning of slaves had grown to become a major moral, political and economic consideration destined to effect the history of the nation.

Free Negro colonists. There are no reliable records of the number of free blacks in the colonies before the Revolutionary War, but undoubtedly many who came to America as indentured servants had served out their bond by that time. Even after the Revolution, during which the morality of slavery was questioned, there were relatively few compared to the total population—but there were more than most history books lead us to believe. According to the first United States census in 1790, there were 59,557 free Negroes in the country; 13,059 in the New England colonies; 13,975 in the Middle colonies; and 32,523 in the Southern colonies.

The increase of the free Negro population was brought about in several ways. In addition to those indentured servants who earned their freedom, hundreds were manumitted for their service in the Revolutionary War. The mulatto children of slave women were often raised as free persons by the white slave owners. Many slaves fled the plantations of the South to re-establish themselves as free men and women in their own colonies. And anti-slavery sentiment caused some colonies to free their slaves by decree.

The legal status of the free black colonist was never clearly or uniformly defined. He was not a slave, yet it was constantly made clear to him that he was not equal to a white person. Free Negroes were even allowed to have slaves—as long as they were not white. In some colonies they were forbidden to fraternize with slaves or whites, in some they were prohibited from bearing arms or joining the militia, and in others their freedom was limited by a network of legal restrictions of their civil rights and personal movement.

The economic position of free blacks was also insecure. As workers, they were not employed where slave labor was available; and as professionals or artisans they were not readily patronized by whites. In the early colonial years, many were forced to work on plantations and farms alongside slaves, or to take whatever menial work they could get, to avoid becoming derelicts and vagabonds.

The gradual industrialization and urbanization of the country opened new opportunities for free blacks. In the towns and cities they were able to find work as shoe makers, coopers, carpenters, cabinet makers, wheelwrights, bricklayers, tanners, and other skilled craftsmen. With increased incomes and less free time, working-class whites sought their services as barbers, tailors, caterers, handymen, and part-time housemen or cleaning women. Iron factories and foundries began employing them as forgemen, firemen and helpers.

Though exerting little influence in the political life of the colonies, free blacks were often able to rise to high social position and financial independence, particularly in the North and Middle colonies. A few were able to open shops and businesses of their own; others administered to the needs of their people as preachers, doctors, and teachers. Many not only learned to read and write, but also made contributions to the cultural and intellectual life of the budding society. A Hessian officer in 1778 wrote in his journal that there were "many families of free Negroes, who live in good houses, have property and live just like the rest of the inhabitants."

Prince Hall, born free in 1735, became a skilled leather worker and property owner in Boston.

CHRONOLOGY OF RELEVANT EVENTS

1400s. Portuguese and Spanish explorers bring the first African slaves to South America and the West Indies.

1492. *Oct. 12:* Columbus discovers America; blacks reportedly in his crew.

1502. European-born blacks accompany Ovando to Hispanola; he later requests white slaves because blacks join Indians and cause trouble.

1512. Blacks arrive in America with Ponce de Leon.

1513. At least thirty Africans, including Nuflo de Olano, accompany Balboa across the Isthmus to the Pacific.

1520. The Cortez expedition to Mexico includes 300 Africans.

1525. Blacks in the expedition of Almageo and Volvidas save their Spanish masters from the Indians.

1526. Blacks go with Lucas de Ayllón as far as Virginia; later revolt and join Indians.

1527. Estevanico, a black guide for Narváez, lands in Florida.

1539. Estevanico heads the party of Friar Marcoz de Niza to explore what is now Arizona and New Mexico.

1542. Juan Rodriguez Cabrillo lands at Santa Barbara, Cal. with party including blacks.

1565. Africans in the expedition of Don Pedro Menendez de Aviles help found St. Augustine, Florida.

1609. Eleven Africans are in the Dutch expedition of Henry Hudson exploring around what is now upper New York.

1619. Twenty Africans are sold in Jamestown as indentured servants.

1624. Two of the "Jamestown twenty" are married and later become the parents of reportedly the first black child born in English America.

1634. Three blacks are with the expedition of Cecilius Calvert landing north of the Potomac River.

1653. Virginia decision won by Negro slave owner, Anthony Johnson, over his slave, John Casor, establishes chattel slavery in that state.

In the sixteenth and seventeenth centuries, blacks were with the French and Dutch explorers.

1657.   Africans and Indians destroy houses of their masters in Hartford and attempt to escape into the forest.

1660s.   Maryland and Virginia make legal distinctions between blacks and whites; Virginia repeals law enfranchising blacks who converted to Christianity and prohibits free blacks from having white indentured servants. Connecticut bars blacks from military service; Massachusetts decrees children of slaves may be sold, classifying slaves as all "Negroes, Moors, Mollatoes or Indians"; forbids whites to trade with blacks.

1661.   New York black slaves petition for freedom.

1663.   Conspiracy of black slaves and white indentured servants is betrayed by house servant in Virginia.

1673.   Marquette and Joliet enlist French and African workers for their exploration of Louisiana Territory.

1687.   Slave plot to kill whites uncovered in Virginia.

1688.   Pennsylvania Quakers make first organized white anti-slavery protest.

1690.   Insurrectionary plot of Indians and blacks uncovered in Newbury, Massachusetts.

1696.   Mayor of New York assaulted by a group of slaves.

1700.   By the end of the seventeenth century, most of the Middle and Southern colonies have evolved slave codes defining their sub-human status, restrictions of liberties, and severe punishments for offenses.

1700s.   Englands victory over France (1713) gives her control of the profitable slave trade; slave importation to colonies increases from 2,500 yearly to 7,500 by 1750; slave codes strengthened to cope with increased resistance and runaways. Slave revolts increase, occuring in New York (1712, 1740 and 1741), South Carolina (1720, 1730 and 1739), Boston (1723), Virginia (1727, 1730), Louisiana (1730) and New Jersey (1741).

1765.   Jean Baptiste Pointe de Sable, black trader, arrives in Midwest with French explorers.

1770.   Quakers open a school for Negroes in Philadelphia.

1773.   First Negro Baptist Church is organized at Silver Bluff, S.C.; Phillis Wheatley's book "Poems on Various Subjects" is published; Patrick Henry, soon after making his famous liberty-or-death speech in Congress, writes a friend: "Would anyone believe that I am master of slaves of my own purchase? . . . I will not, I cannot justify it . . . I believe a time will come when an opportunity will be offered to abolish this lamentable evil . . ."

1774.   *October:* Suggestion is made to the Provencial Congress that "While we are attempting to free ourselves . . . and preserve ourselves from slavery, that we also take into consideration the . . . negro slaves in this province."

1776.   At least two Negroes—a man and a four-year-old girl—are members of the De Anza settlement at what is now San Francisco.

THE PEOPLE

Supporting the fact that many unknown Africans participated in the exploration and settlement of America are the names of the many who, thanks to unbiased early historians, are part of our recorded history. Dredged from scanty records and scattered sources, the evidences of their presence, whether in writing or pictures, are small but important pieces in the mosaic of our early history.

When Christopher Columbus embarked on his first voyage in 1492, he carried as his pilot, Pedro Alonso Niño, who is believed to have been a Moroccan black. On his fourth voyage in 1502 he carried with him a black cabin boy, Diego el Negro.

Three blacks—Francisco Peres, Mathias De Sousa, and John Prince—were in the party that landed around Maryland in March, 1634. Jean Baptiste Pointe de Sable arrived in the Midwest with the French explorers in 1765 and in 1779 established a settlement which eventually became the city of Chicago. In the Northwest, Markus Lopeus, a black crew member of the sloop *Lady Washington* was among those killed when a party came ashore on August 16, 1778 in what is now the state of Oregon. When the British ventured up the Columbia River in 1845 they found already settled there one James D. Saule—also known as De Saule and Saulos—a black sea cook of a ship wrecked near there some years before.

The Spanish explorer Coronado, who is generally credited with the discovery of Arizona and New Mexico in 1540, was actually preceeded by the black guide and explorer Estevanico. Known also as Estevan or Little Stephen, Estevanico had landed with a Spanish party in Florida in 1528, and for the next ten years or more guided the gradually dwindling party across the Gulf states, the northern part of Mexico and Texas, and almost to the Pacific Ocean before being killed in the virgin Southwest territories in 1539.

As the small settlements grew into villages and towns, and farms and plantations sprang up, the names of blacks, both slave and free-born, began to appear, verifying their presence and participation in the life of the colonies. Richard Johnson, a black carpenter, came to the New England colony as an indentured servant in 1651, and after earning his freedom in three years, imported white indentured servants of his own. Scattered throughout the colony were black property owners: Benjamin Doyle with 300 acres in Surrey County in 1656; John Harris with 50 acres in New Kent County in 1668; and Phillip Morgan with 200 acres leased from York County.

As early as 1740 there was a black physician in Pennsylvania, advertised as qualified to "bleed and draw teeth". Near the end of the century there were others, among them James Derham of Philadelphia who had learned medicine from his various physician owners. A South Carolina slave named Cesar developed a series of cures for poisons and was granted his freedom and an annuity of one hundred pounds for his discoveries. A 1773 newspaper advertised a "Negro Artist . . . (who) takes faces at lowest rates."

Outstanding for his talents as essayist, inventor, mathematician and astrologer was the "sable genius", Benjamin Banneker, who also published a popular almanac in his later life. Also known for their writings were Jupiter Hammon, poet and Baptist preacher of Long Island who was the first American black to publish his own verse; and Phillis Wheatley, a slave girl of Boston. Miss Wheatley published her first poems in 1770, and during the War wrote a poem for General Washington who complimented her on her "style and manner".

The religious bodies—Quakers, Baptists, Methodists and Presbyterians—offered blacks the first and greatest opportunities for relative social freedom. Among these were Jacob Bishop who was made pastor of the (white) Baptist church of Portsmouth, Virginia; and William Lemon who manned a white pulpit in Gloucester. Henry Evans and Ralph Freeman of North Carolina; Andrew Bryan of Savannah, Georgia; Black Harry of St. Eustatius; Thomas Paul of Boston; Richard Allen, Absalom Jones and Harry Hosier of Philadelphia; and Lemuel Haynes who became known throughout New England—all both gave and received inspiration in white churches. George Liele founded the first Baptist church in Savannah when that city was under British rule. After the War, most of these men went on to found black churches of their denomination in an effort to enjoy that freedom of worship which had led many of their white countrymen to these shores.

Estevanico

(c.1500-1539)

EXPLORER OF THE SOUTHWEST

His belief that he had found the Cities of Gold inspired Coronado's expedition two years later.

guides, headed his group westward around the Gulf Coast. Crossing the Mississippi River around New Orleans, the leader and many of his men were swept overboard, and within a year most of the rest of them were dead from disease, starvation or Indian arrows.

Estevanico, also known as Esteban or Little Stephan, and three others struggled to east Texas where they were captured and made slaves, each to a separate tribe of Indians. After six years of captivity they met again at a tribal convention and, as a group, managed to escape. For a year they wandered west and south before reaching the Gulf of California to become the first men to cross the American continent. Here a company of Spanish soldiers found them near naked and half dead, and in 1536 took them to the Viceroy of the Spanish settlement in Mexico City.

During their long journey across Texas they had been told by many of the Indians of a fabulous empire abounding in gold and jewels called the Seven Cities of Cibola. Upon hearing these tales, the Spanish Viceroy persuaded Estevanico in 1539 to act as guide for a search expedition headed by one Friar Marcos. Estevanico was instructed to push ahead of the party with a small band of Indians and to send back crosses varying in size according to the riches he found. Within four days, an Indian runner returned with a cross as tall as a man, and, after receiving a second cross, Friar Marcos set out to join his "black Mexican".

But, crossing southeast Arizona, Estevanico had already entered into a Zuni Indian pueblo in New Mexico. Three days before reaching the area where they were supposed to meet, the friar learned from two wounded Indian runners that the Zuni had killed the rest of the scouting party, including Stephan.

Less then fifty years after Columbus "discovered" America, Estevanico, native of a Moroccan village on the northwest coast of Africa, "discovered" the territories in and around Arizona and New Mexico.

Estevanico came to the New World in 1527 headed for Florida with a Spanish expedition of five ships and 506 men hoping to conquer the land and find great quantities of gold. Before they reached their destination in 1528, desertions and hurricanes had reduced their party to four hundred men. Finding no gold, Narvaez, the leader, split the group into two parties and, with Estevanico as one of the chief

Russell Adams, *Great Negroes Past and Present* (Chicago: Afro-Am, 1969). William Loren Katz, *Eyewitness: The Negro in American History* (New York; Pitman, 1967).

Mathias Sousa

MARYLAND SETTLER

Among the original settlers of what is now the state of Maryland was Mathias Sousa, a black indentured servant who later became one of its most distinguished citizens.

Sousa and two other blacks, Francisco Peres and John Price, landed north of the Potomac River in March, 1634 with a party of some 300 "laborers and gentlemen" to settle land granted to Lord Baltimore. Like most of the laborers, Sousa's passage had been arranged according to a formula of Lord Baltimore to encourage settlement of the colony. For every five men between the ages of sixteen and sixty transported to the colony, the expedition leader was to be granted 2,000 acres of land. Sousa worked for two Jesuit priests until he paid off the cost of his passage; he then was given fifty acres of land, tools and three suits of clothes.

Not much is known about Sousa's early life. The first record of him is found in the land claims filed by Father Fisher for transporting him to Maryland. In a number of colonial documents he is found variously referred to as Sousa, de Sousa, Touse, Tousa and Cause. He had apparently earned his freedom by 1641, because in that year he was listed as a member of the Maryland assembly; only free men were given that privilege.

In the fall of 1642, he was licensed to trade with the Indians, and established a reputation as a competent trader whose tact in dealing with the Indians gave him an edge over his Virginia competitors. His understanding of the Indians was also important because many of the Indians in the area were hostile to settlers and traders.

Soon afterward, a ship owner named Alexander Pulton gave Sousa command of a small boat and authorized him to hire a crew for trading with the

Susquehanna tribe. The mission must have had its moments of danger because Sousa wrote of a crewman's bravery that saved "the pinnace and men . . . from disaster by Susquehannonks". Sousa later became a planter in the new colony and, in 1641, as a member of its assembly, helped enact the laws by which it was governed.

Phillip T. Drotning, *Black Heroes In Our Nation's History* (New York: Washington Square Press, 1970). George Reasons, *They Had A Dream* Vol. II (Los Angeles: L.A. Times Syndicate, 1971).

Amos Fortune

(c. 1710-1801)

PRINCE, SLAVE AND FREE MAN

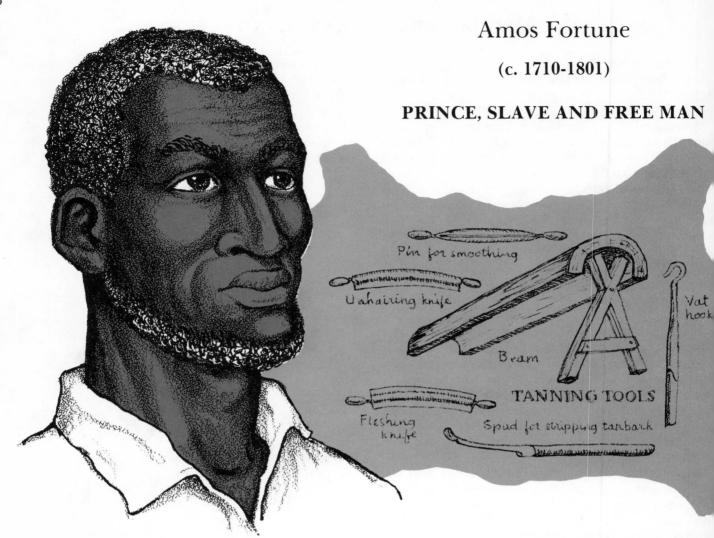

Pin for smoothing

Unhairing knife

Beam

Vat hook

TANNING TOOLS

Fleshing knife

Spud for stripping tanbark

Amos apparently was unable to do this because he was still in the service of the Richardsons more than four years later.

On May 9, 1769 Mrs. Richardson released him from further bondage but he continued to run the tannery for her while he built his own home, established his own business and became an accepted citizen of Woburn. He must have earned a fair sum in 1775, 1778 and 1779 he purchased the freedom of female slaves for marriage, the first of whom died. With his third wife and her child, he journeyed to Jaffrey, New Hampshire, carrying all his belongings and the tools of his trade—spud, barking mallet, rollers, knives, beam and work table.

On the bank of a brook, Amos built a house, a barn, and a tanyard, and established a prosperous business which enabled him to become a landowner by the end of 1789, fulfilling a life-long dream. He was admitted to the white church and lived, honored and respected by all, to the age of ninety-one. A stone tablet honoring this African prince, slave and Afro-American citizen may still be seen in a Jaffrey cemetery.

Captured by slavers in 1725, At-mun, young son of a chief, was brought from his African village and across the Atlantic on the slave ship *White Falcon* to be sold at auction in the slave markets of pre-revolutionary Boston.

The black prince was renamed Amos by the Quaker family of Caleb and Celia Copeland who purchased him, and who, during the fifteen years of his servitude, taught him how to read, write, and weave. He was also promised his freedom, but when his master died in 1740, he was sold along with household articles to help settle the debts of the estate. He was bought by Ichabod Richardson, a leather tanner of Woburn, Massachusetts who taught him the tanning trade.

On December 30, 1763, Richardson drew up a document that granted Amos "full liberty . . . equal to men that are freeborn" at the end of four years, "for diverse and good reasons". It turned out that the "diverse and good reasons" was an agreed sum of money to be paid into a fund over a four year period.

Elizabeth Yates, *Amos Fortune, Free Man* (New York: E.P. Dutton, 1961).

Richard Stanup   (1748-1862)

THE PRESIDENT'S MAN

(The slave accompanying Washington in this engraving is not identified as Stanup.)

In spite of their lowly position, slaves often exerted a moral and emotional influence on their owners. And their less-than-human status did not prevent their development into dignified men and women, nor condemn them all to short and meaningless lives.

Richard Stanup, a slave of George Washington, led a full life—and lived for more than one hundred years! Born in Fredericksburg, Virginia, the son of an unknown slave woman, he was given the name Richard by the then sixteen-year-old George. It is said that the surname Stanup came from the habit of Richard's mother reminding him to "Stand up!" in the presence of his young master. As a young man, Richard helped his master explore and survey the Ohio region, and to determine the state's present boundaries. He also accompanied Washington during the Indian wars, and was with him at several decisive battles of the Revolutionary War. It was during one of these battles that he received a sabre wound, the scar of which he carried the rest of his life.

He grew up to be a big, erect man, over six feet tall, and became one of Gen. Washington's personal servants and bodyguards, and finally his chief in charge of other servants.

As Washington lay dying in December, 1779, Stanup, it is reported, was standing at the foot of the bed. Records show that Washington acknowledged the presence of his body servant Christopher who was standing near, so it is possible that several servants were there even though they were not listed with the four official witnesses of the President's death.

Another slave, William Lee, apparently enjoyed greater favor from the President than Stanup. In his will, Washington granted William immediate freedom and an annuity of thirty dollars for life as testimony of his attachment, and for his faithful service during the Revolutionary War. The freedom of his other slaves, including Stanup, was provided for after the death of Mrs. Washington.

Stanup was awarded 400 acres of land in Champaign County, Ohio; and he claimed ownership of a certificate in Washington's handwriting attesting to their close relationship. He moved to Ohio where he became a preacher and farmer, and lived to the age of 114.

"Richard Stanup Who Had Charge of George Washington's Slaves," *Negro History Bulletin* (Feb. 1969). "More About Richard Stanup, George Washington's Chief of Servants," *Negro History Bulletin* (May, 1969).

Phillis Wheatley

(1753-1784)

COLONIAL POET

One of the first and most publicized victims of the colonial slave trade to disprove the claim that slaves were incapable of learning was the poet Phillis Wheatley. Kidnapped from Africa at the age of eight, she was brought to Boston in 1761, a sickly child only able to speak Senegalese. At the age of thirteen she wrote her first poem; and in 1773 her first book of poems was published, the second volume of poetry published by a woman in America.

At the Boston slave mart, Phillis was purchased by John Wheatley, a tailor whose wife, impressed by the forlorn child's aptitude, taught her to speak, read, and write English. In a few years Phillis had also learned geography, history, and Latin, and had developed a liking for the classic Romantic poets such as Horace and Virgil. Her first poem, a translation from the *Latin of Ovid*, so amazed the literary circles in Boston that they had it published. In 1768 she wrote "To the King's Most Excellent Health", and in 1772 she composed a poem to her mistress who was so moved that she freed Phillis and sent her to England to help regain her health.

With the London publication of her book, "Poems On Various Subjects, Religious and Moral", her fame spread on both sides of the Atlantic, and she became a celebrity. She was entertained by nobility, and the lord mayor of London presented her with a copy of Milton's "Paradise Lost". Abolitionists pointed to her as proof that all Negroes should be freed. In 1775 she wrote a poem to Gen. George Washington and sent it to him. He thanked her for her praise, and invited her to visit him at his Cambridge headquarters which she did shortly afterward.

Despite the kindness of her master and mistress and the affection and fame which she enjoyed, Phillis never liked being a slave. She spoke of her love for freedom in a poem dedicated to the Earl of Dartmouth, ending in these words: "And can I then but pray, Others may never feel tyrannic sway?" Her last poem, "Liberty and Peace", was published the year of her death, a fitting symbol of her aspirations in life.

Russell Adams. *Great Negroes Past and Present* (Chicago; Afro-Am Publishing, 1969). Fishel and Quarles, *The Black American* (Illinois; Scott, Foresman & Co, 1967).

Lemuel Haynes

(1753-1833)

NEW ENGLAND MINISTER

Among the most popular preachers in New England in the Revolutionary era was a former minuteman who was born of an African father and white mother in Hartford, Connecticut. Although he gained distinction in later life as the first Negro to serve regularly as a pastor to white congregations, his early life is also important as an unique example of the varied colonial black experience.

Haynes never knew his father who, as a slave, was forbidden to marry across the color line. His mother was a hired girl, possibly an indentured servant, who worked for neighbors of Deacon Rose of Granville, Massachusetts. Lemuel saw his mother a few times before she died, but she refused to admit or indicate that he was her natural son. From the age of five months, Lemuel was raised by Deacon David Rose who, though blind, gave his young slave the advantages of an education in the district school and instructions in the Christian religion. It became the custom for Lemuel to read a sermon of some noted English evangelist to the Deacon every evening before the Sabbath. One day Lemuel read a particularly impressive sermon which the Deacon could not identify. When he asked Lemuel whose work it was, Lemuel said nothing for a while. Then in a quiet voice, he answered, "It's Lemuel's sermon".

His career in the ministry, for which he was so obviously intended, was postponed by the Revolutionary War. He was a minuteman in 1774 at the Battle of Lexington, joined the Continental Army at Roxboro, and was with the Green Mountain Boys in the capture of Fort Ticonderogo. After leaving the army he began the serious study of theology. He studied Latin and Greek, and received the degree of A.M. from Middebury College in Connecticut.

Licensed to preach in 1780, Haynes appeared before all-white congregations in Connecticut, Vermont, and New York. The climate of freedom and independence he experienced must have taken root; during the War of 1812 he was an outspoken critic of the anti-Federalists who wanted to secede from the Union.

W.H. Morse, "Lemuel Haynes", *Journal of Negro History*, (Jan. 1919). William Simmons. *Men of Mark* (New York; Arno Press, 1968).

Jean Baptiste Point DeSable

(1745-1818)

CHICAGO'S FIRST SETTLER

Unlike most who came to the new world for either adventure or a new life, Jean Baptiste Point DeSable was both explorer and settler. He came from France to the French settlement of New Orleans in 1765 to expand his father's business which was headquartered in Haiti. Before his death, he had explored the Mississippi and water routes as far north as Canada, had established residence in several Midwest towns, and had become Chicago's first settler.

DeSable was born in St. Marc, Haiti, the son of a French merchant father and African mother. He was sent to France for his education, and from there to New Orleans where he stayed only a short while before moving to the newly founded settlement of St. Louis, Missouri. With a French companion, he developed a thriving trading business, but in 1767 moved to Peoria, Illinois to improve his trading contacts with the Indians.

After marrying an Indian and living with the Peoria and Potowatomi tribes for two years, he began exploring the Illinois and Des Plaines rivers and Lake Michigan, eventually setting up trading posts along the trails to what is now Chicago, Detroit and southern Canada.

In 1772, he decided to move his operation to the banks of the Chicago River, and in 1774, having finished a suitable cabin, he brought his family and a group of Indians to establish the first settlement in Chicago.

During the Revolutionary War, in 1778, he was arrested by the British who suspected him of being a spy for France, the new ally of the Americans. After being imprisoned for nearly a year, he was cleared and returned to Chicago where he expanded his holdings and his business, and became one of the growing town's most prosperous settlers. By 1796 when DeSable sold his home, Chicago had been acquired from the Indians by the United States, and was destined to become the trading center of the new nation.

Russell Adams, *Great Negroes Past and Present* (Chicago: Afro-Am Publishing Co., 1969).

II REVOLUTION
AND THE WAR FOR INDEPENDENCE

THE PERIOD: 1770-1783

War neither begins nor ends on a certain day in a specific year; its causes go back into the past and its effects stretch into the future. No war is simple, and few have been fought for noble purposes. All wars are judged from at least two points of view. The Revolutionary War, also called the War for Independence, had at least three viewpoints: the British, the Euro-American, and the Afro-American.

The Drift into War

The drift of the American colonies into a war with England was caused more by economic reasons than political differences or desires for social change. After England's victory over the French in 1763, she was faced with a tremendous war debt, and over the next ten years passed a series of restrictive laws and tax measures designed to raise money from the American colonies. The severities of British rule particularly offended the "lower classes"—small farmers, shopkeepers, artisans, frontiersmen, indentured servants and slaves—and led to protests and open hostility. The major casualties of the hostility occured in Boston in 1770 when a "motley rabble of saucy boys, Negroes and mulattos, Irish Teagues and outlandish Jack Tars" clashed with British soldiers stationed there. Five colonists were killed at this "Boston Massacre". The first to fall was Crispus Attucks, a mulatto runaway slave.

Repressive measures by England and rebellious acts of the colonists continued until April 19, 1775, when British troops marched on Lexington and Concord to confiscate alleged military supplies. There they met a group of white and black armed "minutemen"—colonists pledged to fight at a minute's notice—and the "shots heard round the world" were fired. The Second Continental Congress met on May 10, 1775, and recognized that a state of war existed by appointing George Washington commander of the Continental Army, and by issuing a "Declaration of Causes for Taking up Arms".

In the words of this declaration, the colonists had "not raised armies with ambitious designs of separating from Great Britain and establishing independent states." Independence was the radical idea of daring men such as Patrick Henry, Thomas Paine and a few others; it became a necessity rather than a choice when, after the American defeats at Ticonderaga and Breed's Hill, the British refused to negotiate. In August of 1775, Washington fielded an army of 14,000 troops, among whom were many black veterans of the French and Indian Wars as well as soldier-slave minutemen.

A servant joins in the protest against England's tax programs.

IN CONGRESS, JULY 4, 1776.

A DECLARATION
BY THE REPRESENTATIVES OF THE
UNITED STATES OF AMERICA,
IN GENERAL CONGRESS ASSEMBLED.

WHEN in the Course of human Events, it becomes necessary for one People to dissolve the Political Bands which have connected them with another, and to assume among the Powers of the Earth, the separate and equal Station to which the Laws of Nature and of Nature's God entitle them, a decent Respect to the Opinions of Mankind requires that they should declare the causes which impel them to the Separation.

We hold these Truths to be self-evident, that all Men are created equal, that they are endowed by their Creator with certain unalienable Rights, that among these are Life, Liberty, and the Pursuit of Happiness—That to secure these Rights, Governments are instituted among Men, deriving their just Powers from the Consent of the Governed, that whenever any Form of Government becomes destructive of these Ends, it is the Right of the People to alter or to abolish it, and to institute new Government, laying its Foundation on such Principles, and organizing its Powers in such Form, as to them shall seem most likely to effect their Safety and Happiness. Prudence, indeed, will dictate that Governments long established should not be changed for light and transient Causes; and accordingly all Experience hath shewn, that Mankind are more disposed to suffer, while Evils are sufferable, than to right themselves by abolishing the Forms to which they are accustomed. But when a long Train of Abuses and Usurpations, pursuing invariably the same Object, evinces a Design to reduce them under absolute Despotism, it is their Right, it is their Duty, to throw off such Government, and to provide new Guards for their future Security. Such has been the patient Sufferance of these Colonies; and such is now the Necessity which constrains them to alter their former Systems of Government. The History of the present King of Great-Britain is a History of repeated Injuries and Usurpations, all having in direct Object the Establishment of an absolute Tyranny over these States. To prove this, let Facts be submitted to a candid World.

He has refused his Assent to Laws, the most wholesome and necessary for the public Good.

He has forbidden his Governors to pass Laws of immediate and pressing Importance, unless suspended in their Operation till his Assent should be obtained; and when so suspended, he has utterly neglected to attend to them.

He has refused to pass other Laws for the Accommodation of large Districts of People, unless those People would relinquish the Right of Representation in the Legislature, a Right inestimable to them, and formidable to Tyrants only.

He has called together Legislative Bodies at Places unusual, uncomfortable, and distant from the Depository of their public Records, for the sole Purpose of fatiguing them into Compliance with his Measures.

He has dissolved Representative Houses repeatedly, for opposing with manly Firmness his Invasions on the Rights of the People.

He has refused for a long Time, after such Dissolutions, to cause others to be elected; whereby the Legislative Powers, incapable of Annihilation, have returned to the People at large for their exercise; the State remaining in the mean time exposed to all the Dangers of Invasion from without, and Convulsions within.

He has endeavoured to prevent the Population of these States; for that Purpose obstructing the Laws for Naturalization of Foreigners; refusing to pass others to encourage their Migrations hither, and raising the Conditions of new Appropriations of Lands.

He has obstructed the Administration of Justice, by refusing his Assent to Laws for establishing Judiciary Powers.

He has made Judges dependent on his Will alone, for the Tenure of their Offices, and the Amount and Payment of their Salaries.

He has erected a Multitude of new Offices, and sent hither Swarms of Officers to harrass our People, and eat out their Substance.

He has kept among us, in Times of Peace, Standing Armies, without the consent of our Legislatures.

He has affected to render the Military independent of and superior to the Civil Power.

He has combined with others to subject us to a Jurisdiction foreign to our Constitution, and unacknowledged by our Laws; giving his Assent to their Acts of pretended Legislation:

For quartering large Bodies of Armed Troops among us:

For protecting them, by a mock Trial, from Punishment for any Murders which they should commit on the Inhabitants of these States:

For cutting off our Trade with all Parts of the World:

For imposing Taxes on us without our Consent:

For depriving us, in many Cases, of the Benefits of Trial by Jury:

For transporting us beyond Seas to be tried for pretended Offences:

For abolishing the free System of English Laws in a neighbouring Province, establishing therein an arbitrary Government, and enlarging its Boundaries, so as to render it at once an Example and fit Instrument for introducing the same absolute Rule into these Colonies:

For taking away our Charters, abolishing our most valuable Laws, and altering fundamentally the Forms of our Governments:

For suspending our own Legislatures, and declaring themselves invested with Power to legislate for us in all Cases whatsoever.

He has abdicated Government here, by declaring us out of his Protection and waging War against us.

He has plundered our Seas, ravaged our Coasts, burnt our Towns, and destroyed the Lives of our People.

He is, at this Time, transporting large Armies of foreign Mercenaries to compleat the Works of Death, Desolation, and Tyranny, already begun with circumstances of Cruelty and Perfidy, scarcely paralleled in the most barbarous Ages, and totally unworthy the Head of a civilized Nation.

He has constrained our fellow Citizens taken Captive on the high Seas to bear Arms against their Country, to become the Executioners of their Friends and Brethren, or to fall themselves by their Hands.

He has excited domestic Insurrections amongst us, and has endeavoured to bring on the Inhabitants of our Frontiers, the merciless Indian Savages, whose known Rule of Warfare, is an undistinguished Destruction, of all Ages, Sexes and Conditions.

In every stage of these Oppressions we have Petitioned for Redress in the most humble Terms: Our repeated Petitions have been answered only by repeated Injury. A Prince, whose Character is thus marked by every act which may define a Tyrant, is unfit to be the Ruler of a free People.

Nor have we been wanting in Attentions to our British Brethren. We have warned them from Time to Time of Attempts by their Legislature to extend an unwarrantable Jurisdiction over us. We have reminded them of the Circumstances of our Emigration and Settlement here. We have appealed to their native Justice and Magnanimity, and we have conjured them by the Ties of our common Kindred to disavow these Usurpations, which, would inevitably interrupt our Connections and Correspondence. They too have been deaf to the Voice of Justice and of Consanguinity. We must, therefore, acquiesce in the Necessity, which denounces our Separation, and hold them, as we hold the rest of Mankind, Enemies in War, in Peace, Friends.

We, therefore, the Representatives of the UNITED STATES OF AMERICA, in GENERAL CONGRESS, Assembled, appealing to the Supreme Judge of the World for the Rectitude of our Intentions, do, in the Name, and by Authority of the good People of these Colonies, solemnly Publish and Declare, That these United Colonies are, and of Right ought to be, FREE AND INDEPENDENT STATES; that they are absolved from all Allegiance to the British Crown, and that all political Connection between them and the State of Great-Britain, is and ought to be totally dissolved; and that as FREE AND INDEPENDENT STATES, they have full Power to levy War, conclude Peace, contract Alliances, establish Commerce, and to do all other Acts and Things which INDEPENDENT STATES may of right do. And for the support of this Declaration, with a firm Reliance on the Protection of divine Providence, we mutually pledge to each other our Lives, our Fortunes, and our sacred Honor.

Signed by ORDER and in BEHALF of the CONGRESS,

JOHN HANCOCK, PRESIDENT.

ATTEST.
CHARLES THOMSON, SECRETARY.

PHILADELPHIA: PRINTED BY JOHN DUNLAP.

Broadside of the Declaration of Independence published by John Dunlap, the official printer of the Continental Congress. The first part of the second paragraph is the most quoted section of the document

Proclaiming the Declaration of Independence from the State House. Not many blacks were among the celebrators.

A black youth catches the spirit of independence.

The Declaration of Independence

The idea of separating from England gained favor after the outbreak of actual war, and a committee was assigned the work of drafting the declaration. A first draft, written primarily by Thomas Jefferson, was submitted to Congress the latter part of June, but its strong language against slavery offended most representatives from colonies where this supply of labor was necessary to their economy. After two weeks of furious debate and more days of re-writing, the amended Declaration of Independence was adopted on July 4, 1776.

Despite its silence on slavery, it had the quality of eternity because of the profound—though new—propoundments on political and personal freedom. The section that was to touch the hearts and minds of oppressed people throughout the world down through history, and particularly the black colonists, spoke of "self evident truths":

"We hold these truths to be self evident, that all Men are created equal, and that they are endowed by their Creator with certain inalienable Rights, that among these are Life, Liberty and the pursuit of Happiness; that to secure these Rights, Governments are · instituted among Men, deriving their just Powers from the Consent of the Governed; that whenever any form of Government becomes destructive of these Ends, it is the Right of the People to alter or to abolish it . . ."

Blacks were undoubtedly dismayed that, after hearing so much talk about liberty and freedom, the Declaration contained no provision for their manumission; but to those who heard and understood, the promise was implied and hope was kept alive. Two months after the Declaration, Massachusetts issued a proclamation calling slavery "utterly inconsistent with the . . . struggle for liberty"; and within the year several Massachusetts towns abolished slavery. In the years following, Jefferson worked out an elaborate law for gradual emancipation—and removal—of Negroes from Virginia, but neither he nor any of his colleagues ever submitted it to the Virginia legislature.

However, a virile seed had been planted in fertile ground, and the next two hundred years witnessed struggles to reap the full harvest of the "self evident truths" and "inalienable rights" stated in this profound document.

The Battle of Bunker Hill.

The War

The war officially began on May 10, 1775 and ended on September 3, 1783 with the signing of the Treaty of Paris. Armed conflict started at the Battle of Lexington, three weeks before the declaration of war, and ceased in 1781, two years before the final treaty with Great Britain was signed. While blacks shared the spirit of rebellion and the hardships of battle, they had no part in planning or conducting the war.

Only in retrospect does the Revolutionary War seem orderly. The first phase saw Washington fighting a guerrilla war, taking advantage of his familiarity of the land and support of its people to harass the enemy; and avoiding major battles until he could

overcome the problems of recruiting, training, leadership, and supplies. The second phase of the war, marked by the decisive American victory at Saratoga in 1778, found Washington strengthened by a recruitment program—which included blacks—trained officers, a navy and foreign allies, France and Spain. The British, in 1780, were drawn into the Southern colonies by the prospect of weaker forces and stronger Royalist loyalties, and were trapped by the surprisingly competent and courageous Continental Army. Surrounded at Yorktown, Virginia, the British Gen. Cornwallis surrendered on October 19, 1781.

Above: On the right hand side of John Trumbull's famous painting of the Battle of Bunker Hill is shown Lt. Thomas Grosvenor and his slave who has often been incorrectly identified as Peter Salem. In many reproductions of this painting this armed slave has been cropped off. In 1968, the federal government used this section of the painting in its John Trumbull commemorative stamp.

Below: South Carolina Negroes, prohibited from serving as soldiers, accompanied Gen. Francis Marion, the "swamp fox" as servants and laborers. Here Marion entertains a British officer.

Recruitment of Blacks

In spite of their willingness and ability to fight, early demonstrated at Lexington and Concord, blacks were not at first wanted in the army; recruiting officers were instructed not to enlist them, and some of the states sought to discharge those already serving. It was not long before the defeats, the desertions, and the unwillingness of many whites to fight persuaded Washington to change his policy regarding the black soldiers.

There were several reasons for the colonist's reluctance to use blacks in the early part of the war. The enlistment of slaves violated the "property rights" of their owners, the army did not want to become a refuge for runaway slaves, and some officers felt that blacks were just not capable enough. But the main reason was fear. A slave or embittered free black might be very dangerous if trained to fight and armed with a gun.

After the discouraging winter of Valley Forge the official attitude changed, and many methods were used to recruit blacks. For faithful service, some were promised manumission or a bounty of twenty pounds; some were sold to the army by their owners; others were forced to join to exempt their owners from service. Slave owners in New York were given a certain amount of land for allowing their slaves to enlist; and in many states, recruiters were paid as much as ten dollars for signing up any man, black or white.

The recruitment of blacks was a confused issue not only because rules varied from state to state and changed as the war progressed, but also because the practices of state recruiters was often at variance with the policy of the Continental Army. Though there were many local exceptions, the state practices gradually assumed a regional similarity: In the Northern states, free blacks were accepted and slaves were recruited with a promise of freedom for faithful service; in the Middle states, slaves were drafted or sold into the army as substitutes for their owners; in the Southern states, blacks were accepted only in non-combatant roles.

The Black Soldier

Of the 30,000 troops under Washington's command during the war, black soldiers numbered about 5,000. This accounted for only about one percent of the black population, but without them the war would undoubtedly have lasted longer and cost the colonies more dearly. Vast numbers of blacks, free and slave, fought and died in practically all of the major battles of the war. The record abounds with commendations and citations for individual performance and daring; one of the three all-black units, Col. Green's Rhode Island regiment, earned the praise of the French General Lafayette.

Stirred by deep longings for freedom, slaves fled the plantations t join either the British or the American forces.

The New England states with a relatively smal black population furnished more colored soldier than any other section. Of the Southern colonies Virginia used the most, having over five hundred in its land and sea forces. Motivated by a desire fo liberty more pressing and personal than that of any white colonist, black slaves ran away from their owners in droves, some of them joining the British When the Loyalist governor of Virginia called upon indentured whites and slave blacks to join His Majesty's Troops, he succeeded in raising about six hundred men, half of them black. A corp of runaway slaves calling themselves the "king of England' soldiers" continued their fight for personal freedom until 1786, hiding out in the woodlands around Savannah, Georgia.

All blacks entered the army as privates and were seldom promoted. Sometimes they were not ever registered by their names, often appearing on the rolls as "A Negro Man". They suffered the racism of the times: below-average wages, faulty weapons, old clothing, and the poorest of quarters. Varying numbers of blacks in most of the states were in the local

1779 painting of an unidentified black sailor possibly from Bristol County, R.I., and a crew member of the 20-gun privateer *General Washington*.

militia, manning the forts, guarding coasts or protecting military stores alongside their white countrymen. Those who fought in the battles usually served in the Continental ranks for three years or until the war ended. Most served in integrated units, but Rhode Island, Connecticut and Massachusetts activated all-black units.

Generally, the black man's non-combatant role in the army was that of laborer. They hauled the cannons, tended the horses, drove wagons, forged munitions, built fortifications, repaired roads and destroyed bridges used by the British. In the muster roll of one artillery unit in 1782, Negroes were listed as "wheelers, turnwheelers, smiths, sawyers, coopers, painters, and armorers." They also served as cooks, waiters, servants, musicians, foragers and messengers.

Although the Continental Navy had only fifty vessels during the entire war, it was forced to use blacks due to the lack of skilled white seamen available. Free-born and slave blacks served on the ships *Providence*, *Alliance*, *Alfred*, *Boston* and *Ranger*; others served on the hundreds of privateers commissioned by Congress. They did duty as seamen, cabin boys, powder boys, servants, boatswain's mates, gunners, and gunner's mates. Pennsylvania, Massachusetts, and Connecticut used colored marines; while North Carolina, South Carolina, Maryland, and Virginia often used blacks as pilots because of their intimate knowledge of the coastal waters.

Probably the most dramatic use of blacks was in espionage. Many black soldiers served as spies for the American forces, infiltrating enemy lines and scouting enemy action. Others performed in their roles as humble servants and trusted workers, eavesdropping, observing, and reporting troop movements. And many were counter-spies or in the employ of the British. Whether authorized or unofficial, these black spies were just as susceptible to being captured and shot as whites.

The Results

The War for Independence, and the many proclamations for liberty and freedom were not intended to change the growing institution of slavery, so only the soldier-slaves and their immediate families were freed at the war's ending. Even this did not go uncontested; some masters sued to repossess their returning slaves. George Washington himself, although he strongly wished to see slavery abolished, sought to recapture the slaves who had run away from his plantation in his absence. And many white veterans were rewarded with a bounty of a slave instead of money or land.

The war's ending represented a significant victory of the relatively small number of "rebels" or patriots over a more powerful group of wealthy merchants, aristocrats, royalist-minded governors and officials, Anglican clergy, large land owners, and conservative professionals. It brought about radical changes in government and economic practices. But for the mass of black folk, the War for Independence had little or no immediate meaning.

However, the records indicate that thousands of black soldiers were granted their freedom as well as accorded a respect which they had not enjoyed before. Moved by a new interest in humanity, many prominent people spoke out against human bondage. In various localities, anti-slavery societies became a fighting force in behalf of the slaves, and undertook to prepare them for citizenship. The Continental Congress prohibited the importation of slaves, and in 1787 adopted an ordinance which made slavery illegal in the Northwest Territory. Most Northern states either abolished slavery immediately or provided for gradual emancipation.

Whether intended or not, the Revolutionary War generated a spirit of freedom and humanity which eventually touched the lives of not only all blacks in America but people throughout the world.

CHRONOLOGY OF RELEVANT EVENTS

1770. *March 5:* Boston Massacre; Crispus Attucks killed.

1772. Decision in Somerset Case in England makes slavery there illegal, but does not effect slavery in colonies.

1773. *Dec. 16:* Boston Tea Party; colonists board British ships and dump cargo of tea overboard.

1774. Rhode Island and Connecticut pass laws against the importation of Negroes into the colonies, but not against slavery.

Oct.: Congress is asked, ". . . while we are attempting to free ourselves . . . and preserve ourselves from slavery, that we also take into consideration the . . . Negro slaves in this province." The request is not acted upon.

1775. First emancipationist society in the U.S. organized in Philadelphia.

April 19: Battle of Lexington and Concord; black soldiers participate.

May: Committee considering the use of Negro soldiers decides that only freemen should be used because use of slaves would be "inconsistent with the principles that are to be supported."

June 6: Resolution sent to Congress recom mends "that no slave be admitted into thi army upon any consideration whatsoever."

July 3: George Washington takes command o Continental Army.

July 10: Gen. Washington forbids recruiting of "any negro" or "any Person who is no American born."

Sept. 26: Southern states recommend discharg of all Negroes.

Oct. 8: Due to the increasing participation o blacks, American generals agree "to reject al slaves" and "negroes altogether."

Nov. 12: Gen. Washington again orders "Neither negroes, boys unable to bear arms nor old men . . . are to be enlisted."

Dec. 1: Thomas Jefferson denounces slavery i original draft of Declaration of Independence

Dec. 8: News reaches Gen. Washington o British governor's enlistment of slaves; Wash ington allows enlistment of free Negroes.

British newspaper refers to the American rebellion as a costly interruption of the slave trade.

1776. *Jan. 15:* Gen. Washington authorizes the re enlistment of "free negroes who have served faithfully in the Army at Cambridge . . . bu no others."

July 4: Declaration of Independence adopted final draft has excluded all mention of slavery

Aug. 27: Battle of Long Island; black soldier participate.

Oct. 28: Battle of White Plains; black soldier participate.

Dec. 25: Gen. Washington crosses the Dela ware; black soldiers participate.

Dec. 26: Battle of Trenton; black soldier participate.

1777. Vermont becomes first state to abolish slavery Virginia forbids the enlistment of any black without a "certificate of freedom." North Carolina prohibits the freeing of slaves excep for "meritorious conduct."

June 14: Congress adopts the "Stars and Stripes" flag.

Aug. 16: Battle of Bennington; blacks participate.

Sept. 11: Battle of Brandywine; blacks participate.

Oct. 17: Battle of Saratoga; British Gen. Bur goyne surrenders; blacks participate.

Nov. 15: Articles of Confederation adopted by Congress and sent to states for ratification; privileges of citizenship given to "free inhabitants" only.

1778. *Feb.:* Rhode Island authorizes enlistment of slaves.

June 28: Battle of Monmouth; 700 blacks participate.

Aug. 29: Battle of Rhode Island; Col. Green's newly authorized First Regiment of 125 blacks distinguishes itself by "deeds of desperate valor."

Sept. 19: Battle of Bemin Heights; blacks participate.

Dec. 29: Savannah is taken by the British; blacks participate.

1779. *March 14:* As a result of British campaign in the South, Alexander Hamilton, in a letter to Congress urges greater use of blacks, saying: "The contempt we have been taught to entertain for the blacks, makes us fancy many things that are founded neither in reason nor experience . . . But it should be considered, that if we do not make use of them in this way, the enemy probably will."

March 29: Congress urges South Carolina and Georgia to raise a battalion of slaves for which owners will be paid not less than $1,000; the states refuse.

June 30: British Gen. Clinton solicits black soldiers saying: "And I do promise to every Negroe . . . who shall desert the Rebel Standard full Security."

July: Gen. Wayne's victory at Stony Point is helped by work of black spy, Armistead.

Oct. 9: Battle of Savannah; black Haitians from the French Fontages Legion save the French and American armies.

1780. *May:* Charleston captured by the British.

1781. New York promises freedom to all slaves who serve in the army for three years or until discharged. New Jersey prohibits slave enlistment. Maryland resolves to integrate 750 blacks with other troops. Negro troops under Col. Greene fight to the last man at Battle of Point Bridge, New York.

Sept. 18: Battle of Eutaw Springs; blacks participate.

Sept. 30: Siege of Yorktown begins; blacks participate. British garrison at Fort Cornwallis also includes 200 blacks.

Oct. 19: British Gen. Cornwallis surrenders at Yorktown, Va.

1782. *Nov. 30:* Preliminary peace treaty signed.

1783. *Sept. 3:* Final peace treaty signed.

Engraving from a painting by Alonzo Chappel of the struggle on Concord Bridge.

THE PEOPLE

> The story of the Afro-American in the Revolutionary War cannot be told in terms of brilliant military strategies, outstanding leadership or victorious campaigns. Rather, it must be conveyed through sparse records of the many individuals, lowly soldiers for the most part, whose heroic deeds and performance beyond expectation made their names stand out from, and reflect glory upon, the thousands of blacks whose faithful service was almost lost to history.

Careful and painstaking research has turned up the names of hundreds of black soldiers in the rosters of the American forces, only a few of which can be mentioned here.

Early in 1775, a black slave named Prince Estabrook was one of the first American defenders killed at Lexington where Peter Salem, a "freed slave of the Belknap family"; a black private named Pompey; and a slave known simply as "Joshua Boylston's Prince" also saw their first action.

Among the minutemen who harrased the British on their march to Boston were Cuff Whittemore, Cato Wood, Cato Stedman, Cato Bordman, Pomp Blackman, Samuel Craft, and Lemuel Haynes who, along with Epheram Blackman and Primas Black, later participated in the first American offensive at Ticonderoga.

Helping to dig the trenches at Breed's Hill was Charlestown Eads who had joined up at the beginning of the hostilities. He was later assigned to Col. Bigelou's company of the Fifteenth Massachusetts Regiment where he served until his discharge on December 3, 1780. Awaiting the British charge at Bunker Hill were black patriots Cato Tufts, Caesar Dickerson, Sampson Talbot, Grant Cooper, Cuff Hayes, Titus Coburn, Caleb Howe, Seymour Burr, Prince Hall, and two other slaves listed only as Caesar and Pharoh. (Although the policy of excluding slaves from the army was in effect at the time of the Battle of Bunker Hill, the policy obviously was not strictly observed.)

During the battle, Caesar Brown received a fatal wound in the chest; and Cuff Whittemore, the veteran of Lexington, took a bullet through his hat, but, undaunted, paused long enough in the retreat from the hill to pick up a sword from a dead British officer. Peter Salem earned his place in our history by being credited with killing the British commander Major Pitcairn; and Salem Poor earned the citation of his officers for his bravery and gallantry.

At the Battle of Great Bridge, William Flora, a fr[ee] black, got off the last shots at advancing Redcoa[ts] before joining his retreating comrades "amidst [a] shower of musket balls." Two blacks, Oliver Crom[-] well and Prince Whipple, were with Washingto[n] when he crossed the Delaware; and at least on[e] Phillip Field of the Second New York Regime[nt] died at Valley Forge during the bitter winter of 177[.]

One of the two all-black units from Massachusett[s,] the "Bucks of America", was commanded by one [of] the few black officers in the American army, Mi[d]dleton, a noted horse breaker. The Rhode Island al[l] black regiment under Col. Greene "distinguishe[d] itself by deeds of desperate valor" in 1778 befo[re] making their heroic, last-man defense of their com[-] mander's dead body in 1781,

Particularly heroic were the deeds of two black[s] Jordan Freeman and Lambo Latham, at the Battle [of] Groton Heights, Connecticut on September 6, 178[1] where the Americans lost Fort Griswold. When th[e] British Major William Montgomery, leading [the] charge, mounted the walls of the fort, he was kille[d] by Freeman who was armed only with a pike. Aft[er] the surrender of the fort, the American Col. Ledyar[d] was stabbed by an English officer. Infuriated by th[is] cruel act, Latham (known also as Sambo Lathon) ra[n] the Briton through with his bayonet. He immed[i-]ately "received thirty thrusts from the enemy's ba[y-]onets." In the massacre that followed, Jordan Fre[e-]man was also killed.

Jack Sissons took part in the daring kidnapping [of] the British Gen. Richard Prescott in 1777; and th[e] victory of American Gen. "Mad Anthony" Wayne [at] Stony Point in 1779 was made possible by the spyin[g] of the black farmer, Pompey, who was given h[is] freedom as a reward. Another given his freedom f[or] espionage was James Armistead who served Frenc[h] Gen. Lafayette. And Saul Matthews, a Virginia slav[e]

Plaque showing Jordan Freeman at the Battle of Groton Heights about to kill Major William Montgomery.

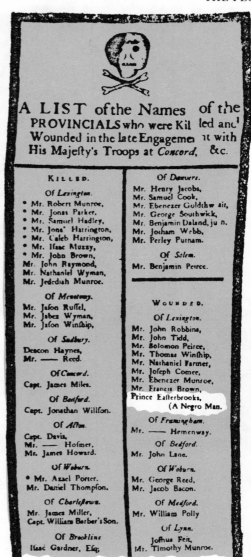

A LIST of the Names of the PROVINCIALS who were Killed and Wounded in the late Engagement with His Majesty's Troops at Concord, &c.

KILLED.

Of Lexington.
- Mr. Robert Munroe,
- Mr. Jonas Parker,
- Mr. Samuel Hadley,
- Mr. Jonas Harrington,
- Mr. Caleb Harrington,
- Mr. Isaac Muzzy,
- Mr. John Brown,
Mr. John Raymond,
Mr. Nathaniel Wyman,
Mr. Jedediah Munroe.

Of Menotomy.
Mr. Jason Russel,
Mr. Jabez Wyman,
Mr. Jason Winship,

Of Sudbury.
Deacon Haynes,
Mr. —— Reed.

Of Concord.
Capt. James Miles.

Of Bedford.
Capt. Jonathan Willson.

Of Acton.
Capt. Davis,
Mr. —— Hosmer,
Mr. James Howard.

Of Woburn.
- Mr. Azael Porter,
Mr. Daniel Thompson.

Of Charlestown.
Mr. James Miller,
Capt. William Barber's Son.

Of Brookline
Isaac Gardner, Esq;

Of Danvers.
Mr. Henry Jacobs,
Mr. Samuel Cook,
Mr. Ebenezer Goldthwait,
Mr. George Southwick,
Mr. Benjamin Daland, jun.
Mr. Jotham Webb,
Mr. Perley Putnam.

Of Salem.
Mr. Benjamin Peirce.

WOUNDED.

Of Lexington.
Mr. John Robbins,
Mr. John Tidd,
Mr. Solomon Peirce,
Mr. Thomas Winship,
Mr. Nathaniel Farmer,
Mr. Joseph Comee,
Mr. Ebenezer Munroe,
Mr. Francis Brown,
Prince Easterbrooks,
      (A Negro Man.

Of Framingham.
Mr. —— Hemenway.

Of Bedford.
Mr. John Lane.

Of Woburn.
Mr. George Reed,
Mr. Jacob Bacon.

Of Medford.
Mr. William Polly.

Of Lynn.
Joshua Felt,
Mr. Timothy Munroe.

The names of hundreds of blacks are hidden in military records, but many are identified by race or by the lack of "Mr." before the name.

ot only obtained valuable information on a British arrison, but led a raid on the garrison that same ight.

Of the many black seamen, Caesar Tarrant, a pilot, nd James Forten, a powder boy, were two whose xperiences were beyond the ordinary. Tarrant layed an important part in one of the rare victories f the American navy; while the young Forten, after ne of the many American defeats, chose to go to rison rather than defect to the British. Performing egular duties were twenty Negroes on the *Royal ewis;* Joshua Tiffany on the *Alliance* with Forten; a oy, Caesar on the brig *Hayard;* Cato Blakney on the *eane;* another Cato (last name was undecipher- ble), a cooper from Boston, on the brig *Prospect;* nd John Moore of Maryland, who was taken pris- ner when the sloop *Roebuck* was captured by the nglish vessel *Dragon.* Many others served on the naller privateers whose rosters were less carefully ept.

Age was no bar to faithful service: Abel Benson of amingham enlisted in the army at sixteen and rved three years; Tony Clark of Billerica enlisted at nineteen and served from 1776 to 1788. Present at Yorktown were two whose longevity was more re- markable than their long service: Jonathan Overton who died in 1849 at the age of 101, and James Robinson who died in 1868 at the age of 115.

A further listing of names would make boring reading, but the tale of Tobias Gilmore must be included for its grim humor. Born an African prince and sold at auction to Capt. Gilmore of Taunton, Tobias entered the war as a substitute for his owner to secure his freedom. For his faithful service, he was also given a piece of land and an old cannon. He began the custom of firing the cannon every Indepen- dence Day until, on one luckless occasion, the patriotic demonstration resulted in a man's arm being shot off. Saying that he "guessed he better stop", he donated the cannon and his uniform to the local historical society where they continued to honor the past less noisily but more safely.

Crispus Attucks

(c. 1723-1770)

"FIRST TO DIE"

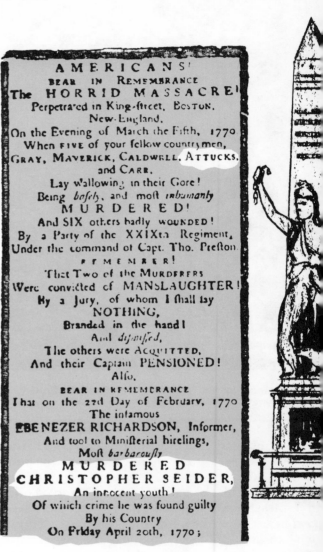

The Boston Massacre was an incident that occurred five years before the official outbreak of the Revolutionary War, but received so much publicity that it came to be considered the unofficial start of the conflict. One of the five "massacred" during the incident was Crispus Attucks, an escaped slave. His death earned for him a place in history as the first martyr to American independence. (Actually, a sixteen year old white youth, Christopher Snider, had been killed by the British ten days earlier.)

Attucks was born in Framingham, Massachusettes, had run away from his owner at the age of twenty-seven, and had become a familiar figure on the Boston docks and in the nearby pubs. The son of Indian and African parents, he was described by his former owner as "a mulatto fellow . . . 6 feet 2 inches high, curl'd hair, his knees nearer together than common."

On the night of March 5, 1770, British soldiers stationed in Boston to protect the unpopular tax officials were goaded and jeered by a group of belligerent colonists. Exactly who or what caused the situation to become violent is confused in the accounts given at the time. A scuffle occured, and the British soldiers, in a moment of panic, fired into the crowd of Americans, hitting eleven. Five died, including Crispus Attucks who received two balls, "one in each chest."

Samuel Adams, prosecuting the subsequent ca[se] against the British soldiers, argued that Attucks w[as] shot without provocation. His cousin, John Adam[s,] defending the soldiers, claimed that Attucks w[as] trying "to be the hero of the night," and that h[is] "very looks was enough to terrify a person." Co[n]flicting testimony was given, but the eye-witn[ess] account of Andrew, one of several slaves in the crow[d,] was the most believable. As to the involvement [of] Attucks, he testified as follows:

"The people seemed to be leaving the soldier[s] and to turn from them, when there came down [a] number from Jackson's Corner, huzzaing an[d] crying, 'Damn them! They dare not fire! We ar[e] not afraid of them!' One of these people, a stou[t]

eral blacks are shown in this engraving of the Boston Massacre. According to eyewitness accounts, the man on the ground or the main figure could be Attucks, who was part Indian and possibly wore his hair long.

man with a long cordwood stick threw himself in nd made a blow at the officer. I saw the officer try o ward off the stroke. Whether he struck him or not I do not know. The stout man then turned ound and struck the grenadier's gun at the cap- ain's right hand, and immediately fell in with his lub, and knocked his gun away, and struck him ver the head. The blow came either on the sol- ier's cheek or hat. This stout man held the ayonet with his left hand, and twitched it and ried, 'Kill the dogs! Knock them over!'

This was the general cry. The people then rowded in, and upon that the grenadier gave a witch back and relieved his gun. And he up with it nd began to pay away on the people. I was then etwixt the officer and this grenadier. I turned to go off when I heard the word, 'Fire!' At the word 'fire', I thought I heard the report of a gun. And upon my hearing the report, I saw the same grenadier swing his gun, and immediately he discharged it.

Q. Do you know who this stout man was that fell in and struck the grenadier?

A. I thought and still think it was the Mulatto who was shot."

Today the name of Crispus Attucks is the first of five carved in the granite and bronze monument erected in Boston Commons to commemorate the historic event.

Russell Adams, *Great Negroes Past and Present* (Chicago: Afro-Am Publishing Co., 1969). William Katz, *Eyewitness: The Negro in American History* (New York, Pitman Publishing, 1967).

David Lamson   FIRST TO CAPTURE

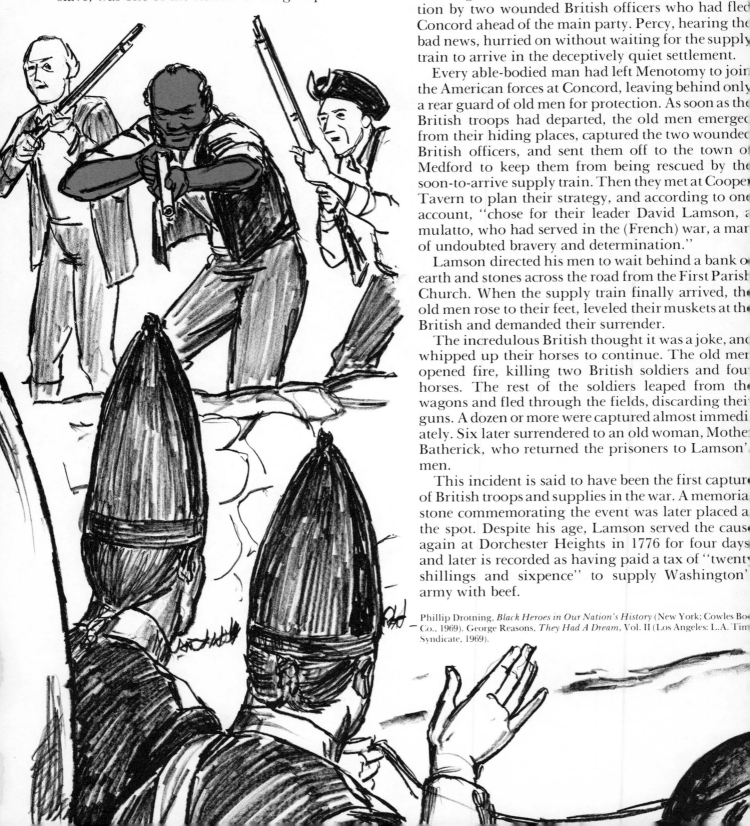

Just a few hours after the first shots of the war were fired at Lexington on April 19, 1775, an incident occurred in the nearby town of Menotomy which made local heroes of a group of men whose age and infirmity would have otherwise kept them out of any sort of military action. David Lamson, an elderly slave, was one of the leaders of the group.

A British relief troop and supply train headed for Concord, and commanded by Col. Hugh Percy, encountered a sabotaged bridge at the Charles River a few miles outside of Menotomy. Instructing the supply train to follow as soon as they could cross the bridge, Percy and his troops entered the town. Here he was given additional details on the British situation by two wounded British officers who had fled Concord ahead of the main party. Percy, hearing the bad news, hurried on without waiting for the supply train to arrive in the deceptively quiet settlement.

Every able-bodied man had left Menotomy to join the American forces at Concord, leaving behind only a rear guard of old men for protection. As soon as the British troops had departed, the old men emerged from their hiding places, captured the two wounded British officers, and sent them off to the town of Medford to keep them from being rescued by the soon-to-arrive supply train. Then they met at Cooper Tavern to plan their strategy, and according to one account, "chose for their leader David Lamson, a mulatto, who had served in the (French) war, a man of undoubted bravery and determination."

Lamson directed his men to wait behind a bank of earth and stones across the road from the First Parish Church. When the supply train finally arrived, the old men rose to their feet, leveled their muskets at the British and demanded their surrender.

The incredulous British thought it was a joke, and whipped up their horses to continue. The old men opened fire, killing two British soldiers and four horses. The rest of the soldiers leaped from the wagons and fled through the fields, discarding their guns. A dozen or more were captured almost immediately. Six later surrendered to an old woman, Mother Batherick, who returned the prisoners to Lamson's men.

This incident is said to have been the first capture of British troops and supplies in the war. A memorial stone commemorating the event was later placed at the spot. Despite his age, Lamson served the cause again at Dorchester Heights in 1776 for four days and later is recorded as having paid a tax of "twenty shillings and sixpence" to supply Washington's army with beef.

Phillip Drotning, *Black Heroes in Our Nation's History* (New York; Cowles Book Co., 1969). George Reasons, *They Had A Dream*, Vol. II (Los Angeles: L.A. Times Syndicate, 1969).

Seymour Burr   FOR FREEDOM

Many slaves, early in the war, were given the chance to decide between immediate liberty with the British or a promise of freedom with the Americans. Seymour Burr was one whose longings for liberty at first outweighed his loyalty to an unproven cause. His change of mind resulted in his being listed in the pages of history as one of the black patriots of Bunker Hill.

Before the war, the fear of slave rebellions had prompted most of the colonies to exclude Negroes from militia service; Massachusetts as early as 1656, and Connecticut in 1660. When the British began recruiting slaves with promises of instant manumission, Seymour Burr, a Connecticut slave, heeded their call and attempted to escape to join their forces. He was captured, but after explaining to his master the reason for his flight, he was promised his freedom he would join the army of the patriots.

Seymour enlisted in the Seventh Massachusetts Regiment and, along with soldier-slaves of the Fifth Massachusetts Regiment, was among the blacks furiously shoveling earth to complete the fortification of Bunker Hill on the morning of June 17, 1775. In the action that followed, the British were driven back twice and lost over 1,000 men before taking the hill. The Americans, who claimed a moral victory, lost less than half that number, including several blacks. Seymour, however, survived not only this engagement but the hardships of the entire war, including the cold weather and food shortage of the siege of Fort Catskill.

At the end of the war, his master, brother of the controversial politician Aaron Burr, kept his promise to free Seymour. It was at this time that he assumed his former master's last name, and as Seymour Burr, settled in Canton, Massachusetts to raise his family.

Wilhelmena Robinson, *Historical Negro Biographies* (New York: Publishers Company, 1967).

Salem Poor

BRAVERY AT BUNKER HILL

Contributors To The Cause...

Salem Poor   *Gallant Soldier*

Bicentennial commemorative stamp issued in 1975.

In answer to a call issued to Massachusetts militia, regiments from nearby towns began to gather on the heights around Charleston on the night of June 16, 1775. About 1,500 Americans, led by Col. Prescott and later joined by Col. Frye and other commanders, began throwing up breastworks on Breed's Hill and Bunker Hill. One of the black soldiers in Col. Frye's regiment was Salem Poor, an ex-slave who had already been in action at Lexington and Concord two months before.

Working frantically through the night, the patriots finished their lines of defense a few hours before the British began shelling the fortifications the next morning. The first assault was launched in the early afternoon, but was repulsed. The Redcoats reformed their ranks and attacked again, and were again driven back. With ammunition running low, the patriots were unable to repel the third charge, and after furious fighting at close quarters, retreated.

Some accounts say that Salem Poor killed Lt. Col.

Abercrombie of the British Regulars. At any rate, in regiment made up largely of whites, he was one of th few who earned a special commendation. A petitio submitted to the Massachusetts legislature on Dec. 1775, and signed by Col. Brewer and thirteen office stated:

"The subscribers beg leave to report to you Honorable House (which we do in justice to the character of so brave a man), that under our own observation, we declare that a Negro man named Salem Poor, of Col. Frye's regiment, Capt. Ame's company, in the battle at Charleston, behaved like an experienced officer, as well as an excellen soldier. To set forth particulars of his conduct would be tedious. We only beg leave to say, in the person of this said Negro, centers a brave and gallant soldier. The reward due so great and distinguished a character, we submit to Congress."

Salem remained in the Continental Army throug the campaign of White Plains on Oct. 28, 1776; an the bitter winter of 1777 at Valley Forge, where th last record of his name is found.

Wilhelmena Robinson, *Historical Negro Biographies* (New York: Publishers C 1967). William Loren Katz, ed., *The Negro Soldier: Missing Pages In Our Histo* (Boston, R.F. Wallcut, 1861. Reprint. Westport: Negro Universities Press, 1970

Peter Salem (? -1816)

BUNKER HILL HERO

1890 illustration shows Peter Salem shooting Major Pitcairn.

One of the true heroes of the Battle of Bunker Hill was Peter Salem, a slave of the Belknap family in Framingham, Massachusetts. As a member of Capt. [E]dgel's company from Framingham, he took part in [th]e minutemen's defeat of the British at Lexington [an]d Concord. Freed, possibly to exempt his master [fr]om service, he joined Col. Nixon's Fifth Massachu[se]tts Regiment, and marched with them to Bunker [H]ill, the scene of the war's first major battle.

Salem's moment of glory came during the third [ch]arge of the British up the incline of Bunker Hill. [T]he Americans were running out of ammunition, [w]hich had included even nails and scraps of iron. [R]emembering Col. Prescott's orders not to fire " 'til [y]ou see the whites of their eyes", the patriots held [th]eir fire until the forward British ranks mounted the [for]tifications.

The British commander, Major Pitcairn, suddenly [ap]peared in front of the colonial lines and shouted, [Su]rrender, you rebels! The day is ours!'' In the [w]ords of one account, ''. . . his commanding air at [fir]st startled the men immediately before him. They [n]either answered nor fired . . . At this critical [m]oment, a Negro soldier stepped forward, and [ai]ming his musket directly at the major's bosom, [bl]ew him through.'' The Negro was reported by an [e]yewitness to be Peter Salem.

Though the Americans were forced to abandon the hill, Peter's comrades were so impressed by his performance that they took up a collection and gave it to him as a reward. He later had the honor of being presented to his commander-in-chief, General Washington. Salem served in the Continental Army until at least 1780, and around 1781 returned to Leicester where he built a cabin and eked out a living weaving cane. He died in a Framingham poorhouse.

Peter Salem's gun is displayed at Bunker Hill with a sign which says: ''Gun belonged to Peter Salem, a colored man, who carried it at Lexington, Concord and Bunker Hill, and with it shot Maj. Pitcairn.''

Joseph T. Wilson, *History of the Black Phalanx* (Hartford: American Publishing Co., 1890. Reprint. New York: Arno Press, 1968). Phillip Drotning, *Black Heroes In Our Nation's History* (New York: Cowles Book Co., 1969).

Barzillai Lew   (1743- ?)

MUSICAL MINUTEMAN

The musical abilities of blacks, which are so often considered a natural talent of the race, were put to use in time of war as well as during the leisure moments of everyday colonial life. Imitating the pomp and formality of the European armies, the American soldiers at first marched into battle to the music of drums and fife. It was not until later that the out-numbered and out-gunned patriots began copyi[ng] some of the guerilla tactics that the Indians used [in] the French and Indian Wars. Thus it was that abo[ve] the noise of shot and shell at Bunker Hill could [be] heard the penetrating sound of a fife played by o[ne] Barzillai Lew.

Lew, a cooper by trade, was born in Chelmsfor[d] Connecticut, but probably migrated to Groto[n], Massachusetts before joining the rebel forces [at] Breeds Hill on June 16, 1775. A giant of a ma[n] loving excitement and adventure, he had served [as] soldier and musician during the French and Indi[an] Wars with the Massachusetts company command[ed] by Thomas Farrington. On May 6, 1775, he enlist[ed] in the Twenty-seventh Massachusetts Regiment an[d] in the company commanded by Capt. Ford, becam[e] famous for his musicianship. In the manner of t[he] painting "Spirit of '76", he, along with other mu[si]cians, kept up a continuous stream of music [to] encourage the embattled patriots at Bunker Hill.

He apparently escaped injury or capture becau[se] later in the war, he organized a band of Negro me[n] all from one family, known as "Lew's men", an[d] engaged in anti-British guerilla warfare in Ne[w] England. It is known that he participated in t[he] action at Ticonderoga in 1777, and some historia[ns] believe that he remained in the army for the duratio[n] of the war.

Wilhelmena Robinson, *Historical Negro Biographies* (New York: Publis[hing] Company, 1967). William L. Katz, ed. *The Negro Soldier: Missing Pages [in] American History* (Boston: R.F. Wallcut, 1861. Reprint. Westport: Negro Unive[rsi]ties Press 1970).

Caesar Bason

BROTHERHOOD AT BUNKER HILL

From its beginning, the Continental Army was so integrated that a Hessian officer of the British army commented: ". . . no regiment is to be seen in which there are not Negroes in abundance: and among them are able-bodied, strong, and brave fellows." Blacks and whites fought literally shoulder to shoulder, and soldiers of one race often risked their lives for individuals of the opposite color. Such was the case of black Caesar Bason and white Capt. Aaron Smith at Bunker Hill.

One of the rearguard under Dr. Joseph Warren protecting the withdrawal of the Americans from the hill, Caesar was hit in the thigh by a British rifle ball just as he raised his musket to fire a parting shot. Unable to flee, he crawled behind a stone fence where he was joined by Capt. Smith of Shrewsbury, Massachusetts. With Bason doing the loading, Smith continued shooting until his musket was smashed by an enemy bullet. Then, lifting the much heavier Bason on his back, he struggled to carry him to safety.

Slowed by his burden, Smith was soon within rifle range of the gaining British. Bason urged Smith to put him down and go on alone. "I'm going to die anyway," Bason said. "You save yourself." Smith tried to get other fleeing Americans to help, to no avail. As a British company drew near, Bason again insisted, "Go, captain, go. Next time you fight, give 'em one for Caesar."

Reluctantly leaving Bason with his wound untreated, Smith, at the last possible moment, fled. One account says that a private Caesar Basom (Bason?) from Westford of Capt. Weyman's company was shot and killed in the trenches. Another says that Bason survived the night, and the next day was one of the thirty American prisoners taken back to Boston and captivity. Regardless of his fate, Bason's belief in the American cause was undoubtedly reaffirmed by the act of brotherhood experienced by him at Bunker Hill.

United Press International, "Racially Integrated Forces Fought at Bunker Hill," *Chicago Defender* (June 14, 1975). William Loren Katz, ed., *The Negro Soldier: Missing Pages In Our History* (Boston: R.F. Wallcut, 1861. Reprint. Westport: Negro Universities Press, 1970).

Oliver Cromwell (1753-1853)

AT THE DELAWARE CROSSING

The black soldier in this engraving of the famous painting by Emanuel Leutze is assumed by many historians to be either Oliver Cromwell or Prince Whipple.

With the same name as an autocratic 17th century ruler of England, a black soldier of the Continental Army established an honorable record as a fighter against autocratic rule in America. The black Oliver Cromwell was born in Columbus, New Jersey, and at the outbreak of the Revolutionary War enlisted in the company of Capt. Lowery of the Second New Jersey Regiment under the command of Col. Israel.

In the fall of 1776, the American army was forced out of New York and New Jersey, and across the Delaware River into Pennsylvania. Discouraged by defeats and the desertion of his troops that winter, Washington knew a victory was needed, and decided on a bold, strategic move. On Christmas night, he marched his ill-clad troops to the ice-clogged river, and in a blinding snow storm crossed the Delaware to surprise the Hessians garrisoned at Trenton. Caught relaxing after their holiday festivities, the British mercenaries had little chance to put up a fight; the Americans suffered only three wounded. The capture of 1,000 prisoners was a great boost to the wavering morale of the weary patriots.

One of the 2,400 who crossed the Delaware on that cold, windy December 25th was Oliver Cromwell. The famous painting of the event depicts a black soldier who the artist may have meant to represent Cromwell or Prince Whipple, another black who was there. Cromwell later saw action in the Battles of Princeton (1777), Brandywine (1777), Monmouth (1778), and Yorktown (1781) where he claimed to have seen the last soldier killed in the war.

After serving "six years and nine months under the immediate command of Washington," he received a federal pension of $96 a year in recognition of his honorable record. A friend said, "His discharge at the close of the war was in Washington's own handwriting, of which he was very proud."

Cromwell settled on a New Jersey farm, and outliving eight of his fourteen children, died at the age of 100. He was buried on the grounds of Broadstreet Methodist Church in Columbus, New Jersey.

Russell Adams, *Great Negroes Past and Present* (Chicago: Afro-Am Publishing Co., 1969). George Reason, *They Had A Dream*, Vol. III (Los Angeles: L.A. Times Syndicate, 1969).

Prince Whipple   (? -1797)

A BOLD BODYGUARD

In May, 1775, a committee of Americans ruled that slaves were not to be allowed in the army. In November, Gen. Washington prohibited the enlistment of all Negroes. Yet, in a contradiction typical of the Revolutionary War, less than six weeks later many blacks were with Washington when he led his troops across the Delaware River. One of them was Prince Whipple, slave of William Whipple, Jr., a planter who later became one of the signers of the Declaration of Independence.

Prince was born of wealthy parents in Amabou, Africa, and at the age of ten was sent to America and treacherously sold into slavery at Baltimore. Prince became a valued and multi-talented servant, and when his owner was commissioned captain in the militia, Prince followed him into the ranks as his bodyguard. At the Delaware crossing and in later campaigns, Prince was always close to his captain in his dual role of protector and servant.

In 1777, Capt. Whipple was promoted to brigadier general and instructed to go to Vermont to stop the advancing army of the British Gen. John Burgoyne. But Prince refused to accompany his owner on this campaign as a soldier-slave: Perhaps imboldened by the colonial spirit of freedom and liberty, or maybe finally realizing the illegality of his status, he asked for his liberation. "You are going to fight for your liberty, but I have none to fight for," he said. Recognizing both the logic of Prince's argument and the value of his service, the general told Prince that if he would continue in military service, "from this hour you shall be free." Prince agreed, and together they shared the victory over Gen. Burgoyne that was the turning point in the war.

After the war, Prince returned to Portsmouth, raised a family, and with his brother established a school for young black children. When he died, "his death was much regretted by both white and colored inhabitants of the town."

Bill Belton, "Prince Whipple, Soldier of the American Revolution", *Negro History Bulletin* (Oct. 1973). William C. Nell, *The Colored Patriot of the American Revolution* (Boston: Robert F. Wallcut, 1855).

Some historians believe this is Prince with Capt. Whipple.

William Flora   (? -1820)

A VIRGINIA VOLUNTEER

(Not a portrait)

While the major action in the beginning of the war involved the forces of Gen. Washington in the Northern colonies, the British also made early attempts to capture several port towns in the southern colonies. In June, 1776, Redcoats were repulsed at Charleston Harbor, and on December 9, 1776, they were unsuccessful at Norfolk. William Flora, a free-born Negro of Portsmouth, Virginia, was among the blacks who volunteered to help in the defense of Norfolk.

The Loyalist governor of Virginia had promised to emancipate all slaves who would join the British Army, but most of the black slaves chose—or were forced—to remain loyal to the American cause. There were also about 1,000 free Negroes of military age in the colony at the time. Like Flora, most of these also chose, of their own free will, to join the American revolutionists.

When the British troops landed and began their invasion of Virginia, Flora was on guard at the Great Bridge outside of Norfolk with other sentinels of Col.

William Woodford's Second Virginia Regiment. Sighting the British, the guards opened fire, more t warn the Americans than to stop the advancin Redcoats. Flora, though only a volunteer sentine was the last to leave the bridge, getting off eight la shots before following his retreating comrade "amidst a shower of musket balls."

The delaying action at the bridge made it possibl for the Americans to organize for guerilla warfar and the troops of Lord Dunmore advanced littl beyond the Great River. They soon were forced t evacuate Norfolk, and withdraw their ships from i harbor.

After the war, Flora was awarded the usual lan bounty of 100 acres, and later became a successfu business man. His loyalty and belief in Americ remained steadfast, and was proven again when, i the War of 1812, he enlisted as a marine on a gunboa

Phillip Drotning, *Black Heroes in Our History* New York: Cowles Book Co., 196 Wilhelmena Robinson, *Historical Negro Biographies* (New York: Publishers C 1967).

Edward Hector (? -1834)

A COOL CONTINENTAL

(Not a portrait)

After defeating the Americans on the east coast in the early campaigns, the British plan for ending the war quickly was to capture the "rebel capital" of Philadelphia where the Continental Congress held its sessions. Marching on the Quaker City, the superior British forces met and defeated the Continental Army at Brandywine in September of 1777. But Gen. Washington withdrew his troops with such skill that he delayed British Gen. Howe's occupation of Philadelphia by two weeks. This delay caused the important capture of British Gen. Burgoyne and his troops the following month.

The orderly and disciplined retreat of the Americans at Brandywine was typified by the conduct of Edward Hector, a black private in Capt. Hercules Courtney's company of the Third Pennsylvania Artillery. Hector was in charge of an ammunition wagon in the regiment of Col. Proctor when the order came down to abandon the wagons. He not only refused to sacrifice the valuable horses, but despite the confusion of withdrawal, went about calmly gathering up the muskets left by his fleeing countrymen. Only then—with horses, wagons, and muskets—did he retire in the face of the oncoming British.

Hector had enlisted in the army just a few months previous, on March 10, 1777. A free man from the relatively liberal state of Pennsylvania, he was probably motivated by the same patriotism that fired his white fellow soldiers. At the war's ending, attempts were made to obtain a pension for Hector but it was not until 1833, a year before his death, that the Pennsylvania legislature granted him forty dollars for his services in the Continental Army.

Wilhelmena Robinson, *Historical Negro Biographies* (New York: Publishers Co., 1967). Leonard Fisher, *Picture Book of Revolutionary War Heroes* (Penn.: Stackpole Books, 1970).

Tack (Prince) Sisson   AUDACIOUS KIDNAPPER

The dark days of the first years of the war were relieved by one spirit-lifting incident—the kidnapping of a British general from under the very noses of his guards.

In the fall of 1776, the American Gen. Charles Lee had been captured, and in order to effect an exchange of prisoners, it was necessary to capture a British officer of equal rank. That summer, Lt. Col. William Barton, in command of the Rhode Island militia,

decided to capture no less than a British general. Among the men he picked for the daring mission was his former slave, Tack (or Jack) "Prince" Sisson. (Some historians believe "Prince" was Prince Whipple.)

Barton put his idea into action when he learned that the British Maj. Gen. Richard Prescott, to escape the heat of the city, had moved away from his troops garrisoned at Newport, Rhode Island to a summer house five miles away. Recognizing the opportunity, Col. Barton and a crew of 35 or 40 men and four officers pushed off in several whaleboats from a spot near Tivertown in Narragansett Bay on July 4, 1777.

For five days they moved stealthily south through groups of British ships and past encampments of Redcoats along the shore until they were within a distance they judged to be three-quarters of a mile from Gen. Prescott's quarters. Reaching a suitable cove around midnight of July 9, they sneaked ashore. Barton discovered that, of the guards on duty, only a single sentry was watching the house. Leaving the rest of the crew to cover his return, he took Sisson and another soldier with him to complete the mission.

Under the cover of the night's blackness, they evaded the guards and overpowered the sentry. Then they burst into the house and charged up the stairs to the General's room. In the words of one account, ". . . the general was not alarmed till the captors were at the door of his lodgings chambers which was fast closed. A Negro man named Prince, instantly thrust his beetle head through the panel door and seized his victim while in bed." The astonished general surrendered meekly and was ordered to dress. However, according to a *London Chronicle* article, he was hustled out of the house "without his breeches."

The three "commandos" with their prisoner stole back to their boats and returned to their lines. The British were greatly embarassed, but the Americans gleefully recounted the event which was "considered an ample retaliation for the capture of General Lee by Colonel Harcourt."

George Reasons, *They Had A Dream*, Vol. I (Los Angeles: L.A. Times Syndicate 1969). Joseph T. Wilson, *History of the Black Phalanx* (Hartford: America Publishing Co., 1890. Reprint. New York: Arno Press, 1968). Wilhelmena Robinson, *Historical Negro Biographies* (New York: Publishers Co., 1967).

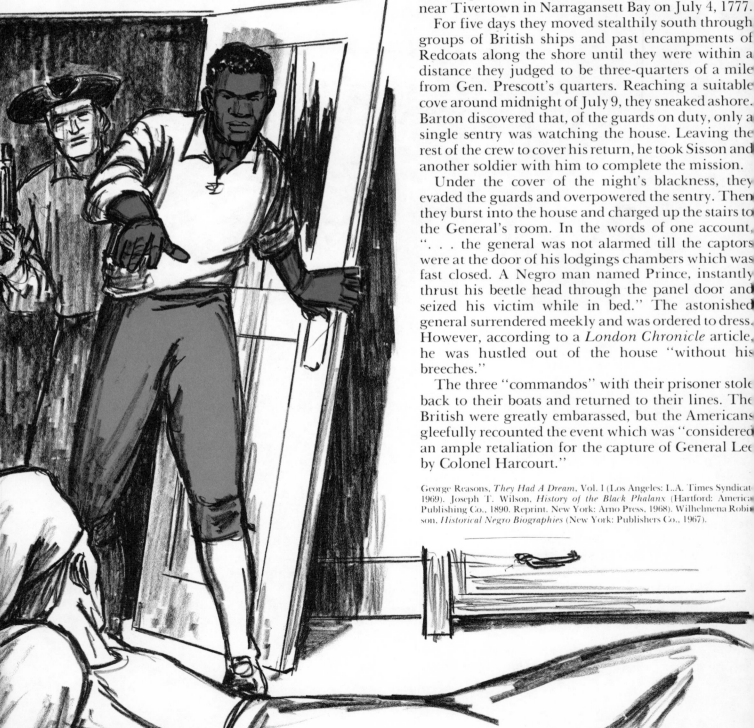

Dick Pointer (? -1827)

FRONTIER BATTLER

The War of Independence was not confined to the thirteen colonies for very long; the pioneers and settlers in the British-owned territory to the west were soon drawn into the conflict. In 1778, George Rogers Clark organized a small army to fight the British and their Indian allies in the Ohio and Illinois territories. In the many isolated frontier settlements too, blacks and whites waged a lonely war.

In May, 1778, a party of two hundred Shawnee Indians approached Fort Donally near Lewisberg, West Virginia, where sixty settlers from surrounding farms had taken refuge. Outnumbered, Col. Andre Donally sent his "powerful, large, very black" slave Dick Pointer to Camp Union ten miles away for help. After returning from the crucial trip, Pointer and another man named Philip Hammond were standing guard in the kitchen of the largest house inside the fort when the Indians attacked just before dawn.

Leaving their guns in a nearby stable, the Indians moved in quietly with tomahawks and war clubs so as not to arouse the sleeping settlers. Then rushing the door of the largest house, they started battering it down. Pointer and Hammond held the door until it began to split, then jerking it open, Hammond shot and killed the first warrior coming through it. Pointer blasted away with a musket loaded with swanshot—a mixture of nuts, bolts, nails and scrap metal—killing several more about to enter.

The shooting aroused the rest of the settlers who drove the Indians off, leaving seventeen of their dead inside the stockade. When Capt. John Stuart arrived from Camp Union the next day, Pointer had already buried the Indians and the four settlers killed.

For his bravery, Pointer was later freed and given a "lifetime lease" on a small parcel of land upon which the grateful settlers built a cabin for him and his wife. He was refused a pension in his final years, but when he died he was buried in Lewisburg with full military honors.

George Reasons, *They Had A Dream*, Vol. III (Los Angeles: L.A. Times Syndicate, 1969).

Samuel Charlton   Austin Dabney

PATRIOTS BY PROXY

Of the Northern colonies, New Jersey, though small, had a slave population second only to New York. And, despite its humanitarian history, it observed customs of slavery similar to its southern neighbors. The case of Samuel Charlton, a New Jersey slave born in 1760, was an example.

At the age of 16 or 17, too naive to understand the issues of the war, he was placed in the Continental Army as a substitute for his master, for which he was rewarded with a silver dollar. He fought in the Battles of Brandywine (Sept. 11, 1777), Germantown (Oct. 4, 1777), and Monmouth (June 28, 1778). For a time he was with the baggage train of Gen. Washington, and was commended by the General for his courage. After the war, he was returned to servitude until, at the death of his owner, his freedom and a lifetime pension was provided for in the will. Upon his liberation, Charlton and his wife moved to New York where he died in 1843.

William G. Nell, *The Colored Patriot of the American Revolution* (Boston: Robert F. Wallcut, 1855).

Most of the colonies practising slavery during the war permitted slaves to substitute for their owners in the militia. One of these substitute (proxy) soldiers was Austin Dabney, a Burke County slave who entered the Georgia militia as an artilleryman.

According to the accounts in the papers of Gov. Gilmer, Austin lived with a Georgia farmer named Aycock, and served in the army in Aycock's place. He was given the name Dabney by the captain of the company he first joined. Few details are given about the battles he fought in; records show that his service ended in 1779 when he was struck in the thigh by a rifleball at the Battle of Kettle Creek, crippling him for life. Near death, he was taken in by a white farmer named Harris who nursed him back to health.

Forty-two years later, the state of Georgia cited Dabney for bravery, granted him an annual pension, and awarded him 112 acres of land in Walton County. He became a respected citizen of Georgia and a friend of Georgia Governor George Gibner who called him a "good soldier" with a conspicuous record of military service.

George Reasons, *They Had A Dream*, Vol. III (Los Angeles: L.A. Times Syndicate, 1969). Leonard Fisher, *Picture Book of Revolutionary War Heroes* (Penn.: Stackpole Books, 1970).

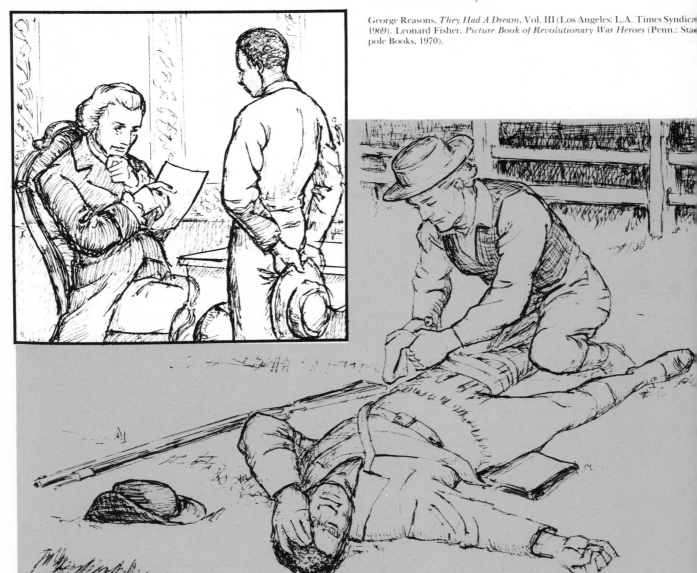

Caesar Tarrant   (? -1796)   SHIP'S PILOT

When the war began, the Americans had no navy because up to this time they had been under the protection of England. The Continental Congress immediately ordered ships to be built, and by the end of 1775 the Americans had a small navy of thirteen vessels plus the ships of some of the colonies. Virginia, which floated the largest of the state navies, used many black pilots; among them was Caesar, a slave of Carter Tarrant of Hampton.

Born in Elizabeth City, Virginia, Caesar entered the service in 1776 or 1777, and served on the schooner *Patriot* under the command of Commodore Taylor. He was at the wheel when his ship engaged and captured the British brig *Fanny,* south of the Cape of Virginia. Caesar was commended for his gallantry and skill displayed during the encounter.

He remained in the Virginia Navy for over four years until the British captured the *Patriot* on the eve of the Battle of Yorktown. Years after the war, on November 14, 1786, the Virginia legislature passed a resolution for his emancipation, stating that "he had entered into the service of his country, and continued to pilot armed vessels of this state during the late war." In 1830, Virginia granted to his heirs land in Ohio set aside for veterans of the Revoluion.

Wilhelmena Robinson, *Historical Negro Biographies* (New York: Publishers Co., 1967). William L. Katz, ed., *The Negro Soldier: Missing Pages In Our History* (Boston: R.F. Walcutt, 1861. Reprint. Westport: Negro Universities Press, 1970).

(Not a portrait)

Joseph Ranger   **AMERICAN SEAMAN**

(Not a portrait)

Few Americans, white or black, were issued complete uniforms.

Black crewmen were used extensively in the gal-lant American efforts, particularly on the Virginia man-of-war vessels, *Patriot*, *Liberty*, *Tempes Dragon*, *Dilegence*, *Hero*, and the *Jefferson*. Josep Ranger, a "free man of color", served on four of thes ships, and had one of them blown out from unde him.

A native of Northumberland, Ranger enlisted i the naval service of the Commonwealth of Virgini in 1776. He saw action on the *Hero* and the *Drago* before joining the *Jefferson* which was blown up b the British on the James River. Surviving this, h came aboard the *Patriot* only to be taken prison when the crew was captured by a British ship short before Cornwallis surrendered at Yorktown in 178 He served the longest possible tour of duty b remaining in the Navy until Virginia disposed of i last ship in 1787.

After being discharged, he received the feder pension of ninety-six dollars a year and a land grar from the Commonwealth of Virginia, possibly in th Virginia Military Reserve of the Northwe Territory.

Wilhelmena Robinson, *Historical Negro Biographies* (New York: Publisher (1967).

Although the American navy did little to threaten the supremacy of the English navy until it was joined by the French, it did keep the British sea forces busy and withdrew some of their strength from the land campaigns.

John Marrant   **BRITISH SEAMAN**

(Not a portrait)

Neither British nor American seamen had regulation uniforms

At no time during the War for Independence were the American goals of "life, liberty and the pursuit of happiness" clearly defined for African-Americans. The slavery issue confused the recruitment policies and status of not only soldier-slaves but free-born blacks as well. As a result, thousands of slaves and many freemen joined the ranks of His Majesty's troops. John Marrant was one of the free blacks who chose to serve in the Royal Navy.

What little is known of Marrant was recorded by a white friend, the Rev. William Aldridge, who wrote a brief account of his life "from the lips of Marrant himself" several years after the war. Born free in New York City, Marrant was raised and schooled in the south. Around 1765, he abandoned a promising career in music to become a frontier preacher and missionary among the Indians.

When the war broke out, Marrant was recruited by the British and served in the Royal Navy aboard the 44-gun *Princess Amelia* for almost seven years. In spite of his religious calling, he apparently felt no guilt at warring with his former countrymen. He recounted a bloody engagement of 1781:

"We had a great number killed and wounded, the deck was running with blood. Six men were

killed and three wounded at the same gun with me. My head and face were covered with the blood and brains of the slain. I was wounded but did not fall til a quarter of an hour before the engagement ended and was happy during the whole of it."

After the war, as if still in pursuit of his happiness, Marrant worked as a merchant and preacher in London, and pastored a church in Nova Scotia, Canada, where Britain had started a colony for her black Loyalist. He came back to America to become chaplain of the first black Masonic lodge, but shortly afterward returned to England to stay.

George Reasons, *They Had A Dream*, Vol. III (Los Angeles: L.A. Times Syndicate, 1969).

Major Jeffrey

HONORARY OFFICER

The Afro-Americans who participated in the war knew that their ancestors were not slaves, so the utterances of liberty by the radical colonists fanned fires of freedom long smoldering in the hearts of the enslaved blacks. The legislature-hall eloquence of Patrick Henry and Samuel Adams spurred many black soldiers to a battlefield bravery that amazed their white officers. In distant Tennessee, a slave called Jeffrey heard the ringing words and was inspired.

During the campaign of Maj. Gen. Andrew Jackson in Mobile, Jeffrey, who had joined up as a laborer, was given the duties of a "regular" in the troops of Major Stump. In an encounter with the British one day, the Major ordered a charge that was met with vicious resistance, and the Americans began to fall back in disorder. Jeffrey, seeing the situation and sensing the disaster about to befall his comrades, rushed forward, seized a passing horse and mounted it. Though only a common soldier, he "took command of the troops, and, by an heroic effort, rallied them to the charge, completely routing the enemy who left the Americans masters of the field."

For his courageous show of leadership, Jeffrey was immediately given the title of "Major", a rank largely honorary inasmuch as, according to the American policy at that time, such a commission was not permitted. In Nashville, where he lived after the war, the story of how Jeffrey earned his title was told and re-told until the day of his death. He was highly respected by the whites generally, and almost revered by his black friends and neighbors.

Ironically, the independent spirit which won him honors in time of war caused his death in the time of peace. Sentenced to a severe flogging for striking a young white ruffian, the seventy-year-old slave died as much from heartbreak as from the beating.

Joseph T. Wilson, *History of the Black Phalanx* (Hartford: American Publishing Co., 1890. Reprint. New York: Arno Press, 1968).

Henri Christophe (1767-1820)

A YOUNG ALLY

In December, 1778, Savannah, Georgia was captured by the British. Less than a year later the Americans and the French allies made an unsuccessful attempt to retake the city. The occasion of the defeat on October 9, 1779, was noteworthy for two reasons: the Americans were saved from complete rout by the rearguard action of black Haitian soldiers with the French troops; among the black soldiers was a young boy who would one day become Emperor of Haiti—Henri Christophe.

Christophe was born on one of the small islands of the West Indies. When he was twelve, he ran away on a French ship which happened to dock at Cap Francois where the French Admiral Charles Hector, Comte d'Estaing was signing up volunteers for the expedition to Savannah. Christophe was sold to one of the French officers as a messboy and bootblack, and accompanied him on the futile Savannah raid.

D'Estaing's army of 3,600 included 545 Negroes officially designated the "Volunteer Chasseur." The French-American forces first tried to lay siege to Savannah, but after supplies began to run short, they decided to attack the strong fortifications. Met by a devastating volley of rifle fire that wounded d'Estaing, the Allies were forced to retreat. The British immediately counter attacked and left their trenches in pursuit of the disorganized Americans, but they ran into the determined delaying action of the black rearguard group under the command of Viscount de Frontage. Some accounts say that Christophe, with the rank of Sergeant, was in the front row and was wounded in the battle, but this is not fully substantiated, and seems unlikely in view of his young age. He was, at least, an eyewitness.

The Haitians "saved the Franco-American army from total disaster by heroically covering its retreat." In the black battalion were several men who later became heroes in the fight for the freedom of their own country—Jean Baptiste Chavanne and Andre Riguard were two—as well as the young Christophe who, as a man still influenced by the principles of the American Revolution, ruled Haiti from 1807 to 1820.

William L. Katz, ed. *The Negro Soldier: Missing Pages In Our History* (Boston: R.F. Wallcut, 1861. Reprint. Westport: Negro Universities Press, 1970). Herbert Aptheker, *The Negro in the American Revolution* (New York: International Publishers, 1940).

Pompey Lamb   **CIVILIAN SPY**

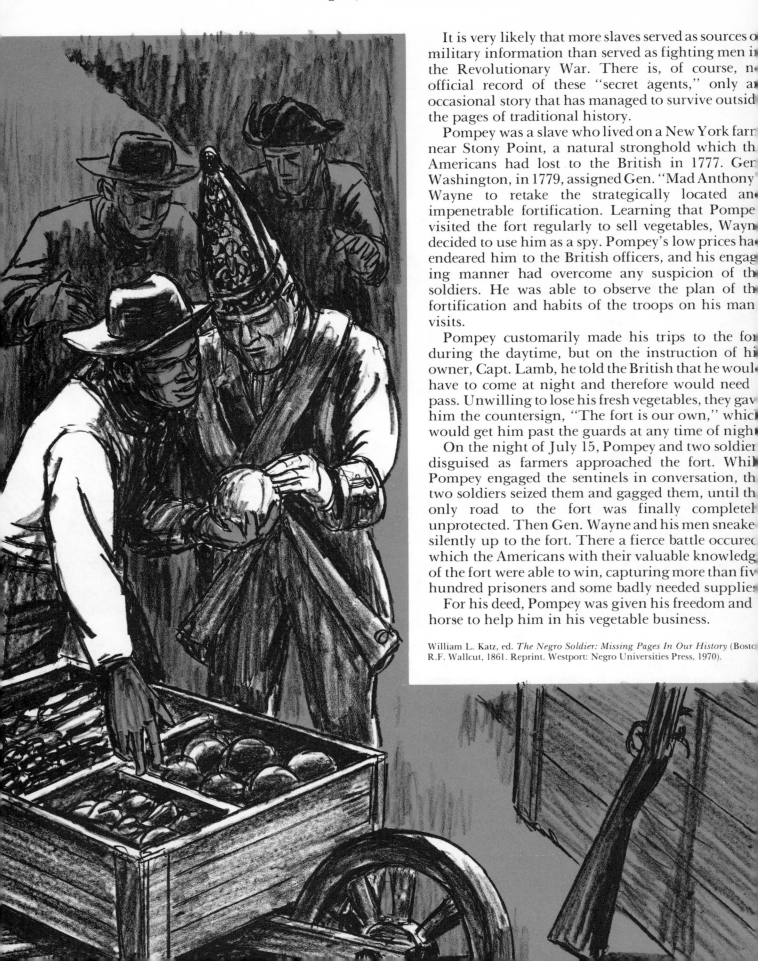

It is very likely that more slaves served as sources o military information than served as fighting men i the Revolutionary War. There is, of course, n official record of these "secret agents," only a occasional story that has managed to survive outsid the pages of traditional history.

Pompey was a slave who lived on a New York farm near Stony Point, a natural stronghold which th Americans had lost to the British in 1777. Gen Washington, in 1779, assigned Gen. "Mad Anthony Wayne to retake the strategically located an impenetrable fortification. Learning that Pompe visited the fort regularly to sell vegetables, Wayn decided to use him as a spy. Pompey's low prices ha endeared him to the British officers, and his engag ing manner had overcome any suspicion of th soldiers. He was able to observe the plan of th fortification and habits of the troops on his man visits.

Pompey customarily made his trips to the for during the daytime, but on the instruction of hi owner, Capt. Lamb, he told the British that he woul have to come at night and therefore would need pass. Unwilling to lose his fresh vegetables, they gav him the countersign, "The fort is our own," whic would get him past the guards at any time of nigh

On the night of July 15, Pompey and two soldier disguised as farmers approached the fort. Whil Pompey engaged the sentinels in conversation, th two soldiers seized them and gagged them, until th only road to the fort was finally completel unprotected. Then Gen. Wayne and his men sneake silently up to the fort. There a fierce battle occured which the Americans with their valuable knowledg of the fort were able to win, capturing more than fiv hundred prisoners and some badly needed supplie

For his deed, Pompey was given his freedom and horse to help him in his vegetable business.

William L. Katz, ed. *The Negro Soldier: Missing Pages In Our History* (Bosto R.F. Wallcut, 1861. Reprint. Westport: Negro Universities Press, 1970).

Saul Matthews   **SOLDIER-SPY**

The state of Virginia, which allowed only free
egroes in its militia in 1777, had lost an estimated
0,000 slaves by 1778. Many of them undoubtedly
sponded to the call of the British royal governor to
elp the cause of England. Others probably fled the
ate for the frontier territories to the west. But great
umbers of them followed the American armies,
rving in whatever capacity they were permitted.

Saul Matthews, a native of Norfolk County, was
mong the Virginia slaves who fought for American
ndependence, serving in the State militia as a rifle-
an for six years. When British Gen. Cornwallis in
781 occupied a position that gave him control of
ortsmouth, information was urgently needed by the
mericans on enemy strength and movements on the
ames River. Col. Josiah Parker, the American com-
ander of the four counties of the area, assigned Saul

to the dangerous mission of obtaining the necessary
information.

Matthews infiltrated the British lines and noted
things in such detail that he was made responsible for
leading a raiding party against the British on the
same night he returned to his lines. The raid was
successful and netted a number of prisoners. The
British, though sustaining only slight losses, were
forced to shift their troops to other positions.

Col. Parker praised Matthews publicly and must
have used him on other occasions as spy, scout, and
soldier. In 1792, the Virginia legislature granted
Matthews his freedom, and cited him for the "many
very essential services rendered to the Commonwealth during the late war."

Wilhelmena Robinson, *Historical Negro Biographies* (New York: Publishers Co.,
1967). Leonard Fisher, *Picture Book of Revolutionary War Heroes* (Harrisburg:
Stackpole Books, 1970).

James Armistead Lafayette   **DARING DOUBLE AGENT**

(The Negro is
not identifie
as James.

**Painting shows British officers visiting headquarters of Gen. Was
ington at Yorktown.**

Many free Negroes in the northern sector of the war, ineligible for regular duty in the army for one reason or another, had the opportunity and motivation to act as messengers, scouts or spies for the American forces. But the boldest spy of all was probably a slave named James who was owned by William Armistead, a planter in New Kent County, Virginia.

After British Gen. Cornwallis established his headquarters in Yorktown in the summer of 1781, one of the blacks seen constantly hovering around the camps was James. According to some accounts, he was soon put on the British payroll for performing various duties, including a bit of spying. When Gen. Washington joined Gen. Lafayette to trap Cornwallis on the peninsula that autumn, the French general was able to supply him with a surprising amount of information on the British troops. Much of this

information from the enemy camp, said Gen. Lafa ette, was obtained by his most valuable agent, Jam Armistead!

During the siege of Yorktown, Armistead was on mission for Gen. Lafayette, and returned to th Frenchman's quarters two days after Cornwall surrendered. A few days later the defeated Britis general paid a courtesy call to Gen. Lafayette headquarters where he was greatly surprised to s the familiar face of his trusted James.

Gen. Lafayette later wrote a commendation to th Virginia legislature stating: ". . . the bearer by th name of James has done essential service to me whi I had the honor to command in this state. H intelligence from the enemy's camp were industr ously collected and more faithfully delivered . . . H properly acquitted himself with some importar communications I gave him and appears to be ent tled to every regard his situation can admit of." Th act emancipating Armistead in 1786 stated that h "kept open a channel of the most useful informatio to the army of the state."

In 1824, when the Marquis de Lafayette visite Richmond, Virginia, he was surprised and pleased i meeting his former spy to find that Armistead ha adopted the name "Lafayette."

George Reasons, *They Had A Dream*, Vol II (Los Angeles: L.A. Times Syndic 1969). Wilhelmena Robinson, *Historical Negro Biographies* (New York: Publ ers Co., 1967).

Deborah Gannett   LIBERATION VIA IMPERSONATION

(Not a portrait)

Deborah Gannett was a woman who served in the Massachusetts Militia for nearly a year and a half without pay masquerading as a man; historians differ on her racial identity. The assumption that she was black is based on the early mention of her in the book *Colored Patriots of the American Revolution* written by the generally-accurate, black, William C. Nell. He, however, includes her story because it was part of the war memories of Seymour Burr, the black soldier who also served in the Massachusetts militia. While not clearing up the question of her race, the story is confirmed in an extract from records of the General Court of Massachusetts for a session in 1791:

"... it appears to this Court that the said Deborah Gannett enlisted, under the name of Robert Shurtliff, in Capt. Webb's company, in the 4th Massachusetts Regiment on May, 20th, 1782, and did actually perform the duty of a soldier, in the late army of the United States, to the 23rd day of October, 1783, for which she received no compensation; and ... it further appears that the said Deborah exhibited an extraordinary instance of female heroism, by discharging the duties of a faithful, gallant soldier, and at the same time preserving the virtue and chastity of her sex unsuspected and unblemished, and was discharged from the service with a fair and honorable character: therefore ... the Treasure ... hereby is directed to issue his note to the said Deborah for the sum of thirty four pounds, bearing interest from Oct. 23, 1783."

Whether white or black, as a woman, Deborah Gannett deserves historical mention alongside Molly Pitcher, Deborah Gilbert, Margaret Corbin and other colonial women who, like Negroes, were denied personal freedom as much by the confines of their stereotyped roles as by their lack of political and civil rights.

William C. Nell, *Colored Patriots of the American Revolution* (Boston: R.F. Wallcutt, 1855). Leonard E. Fisher, *Picture Book of Revolutionary War Heroes* (Harrisburg: Stackpole Books, 1970).

James Robinson   (1753-1868)

BEYOND THE FINAL VICTORY

From the first shots at Lexington to the last battle at Yorktown, Afro-Americans participated in the War for Independence. Not all of them won the freedom for which they thought they were fighting—on either side of the conflict. Thousands who served the British sailed to Nova Scotia, Canada to settle on land granted them by the Crown. Even here they did not find equality; their land grants were smaller than those of white Loyalists, more remotely located, and always separated from the settlements of the whites.

Most of the soldier-slaves of the northern colonies were emancipated as promised, but many black veterans returned to their homes only to resume their former life of servitude. James Robinson was one of these less fortunate.

Robinson was born a slave in 1753, a native of Maryland where a slave code had been instituted by the late 1600s. In 1780, Maryland authorized the recruitment of slaves, with the consent of their owners; and in 1781, when the quotas were not filled, the legislature voted a grant of land to slave holders for each slave enlisted. Robinson was persuaded to enlist on the promise of his master that he would b given his freedom upon the completion of his mil tary service.

It is likely that Robinson joined the Secon Maryland Brigade, which already included Negroe and took part in the Battle of Camden. His conduct a a soldier is suggested in the fact that he was awarded gold medal by General Lafayette for military valor i the Battle of Yorktown. Despite this honor, upon h return home, Robinson was made to serve out h bondage. After the death of his master, the heirs als refused to honor the promise. Instead, they sold hi on the New Orleans slave market.

Like many slaves who first tasted freedom an equality on the battlefield, Robinson never lost th hope born at the Yorktown victory. He fought in th War of 1812, but only gained his long-sought liber through the Emancipation Proclamation of the Civ War—more than eighty years after the victory c Yorktown.

Kent Britt, "The Loyalists", *National Geographic* (April, 1975). Wilhelm Robinson, *Historical Negro Biographies* (New York: Publishers Co., 1967).

Painting shows Gen. Washington accepting surrender of Cornwallis at Yorktown.

(The black soldier on the right hand side of this painting is not iden tified as James Robinson.)

III FOUNDING
AND GROWTH OF THE NATION

THE PERIOD: 1776-1850s

For more than seventy-five years the infant nation experienced acute philosophical and territorial growing pains before reaching its adolescence in the mid-1800s. The sophisticated idealism of its political preachments often conflicted with the immature morality of its practices. But its inherent strength resulted in a surging growth "from sea to shining sea". And black Americans were a factor in the conflicts as well as the growth.

Slavery as a factor in the founding of the nation

The Declaration of Independence—The Declaration of Independence, marking the birth of the new nation, also crystalized the nature of the conflict between the pro-slavery and the anti-slavery groups in the colonies. The debates begun at its writing forecasted the arguments to be put forth throughout the formation of the new government and the expansion of its territories.

The pro-slavery forces, primarily in or from the South, would oppose any effort of the new government to restrict slavery, believing that the economic benefits of its practice would prove its rectitude and guarantee its spread. The abolitionists would fight for specific federal prohibitions of slavery in order to bring the legal and political practices of the nation into line with the moral implications of the Declaration. Both groups would argue their case in terms of national interest, and would attempt to compromise their differences for the sake of national unity.

The Articles of Confederation—Previous to the adoption of the Declaration, steps for the formation of a government by and between the colonies had been taken. On June 11, 1776, a committee of one delegate from each colony was formed for that purpose, and a report was made soon after; but it was not until November 15, 1777, that the Articles of Confederation were adopted by Congress. One of the reasons for the long delay was the issue of slavery. In the consideration of both representation and taxes, long and frequent debates centered around the question of whether the slaves were people or whether they were property and "should not be considered as members of the State more than cattle." The Articles, as finally ratified in 1781, evaded the touchy issue.

The Constitution of the United States—The Articles of Confederation proved weak and unsatisfactory in many other respects, so a Constitutional Convention was convened in 1787 to formulate a stronger plan of government. Again, slavery was a prime consideration. When a House of Congress was proposed, with representation based on population, delegates from the otherwise-humanitarian North argued that slaves were property and therefore did not qualify for representation. The South demanded that (in this isolated instance) the slaves be counted equal with whites. However, when it was further proposed that direct taxes also be based on population, the arguments became confused, and a compromise was made.

In the Constitution ratified in 1798, Article I, Section 2 counted as population all free persons and indentured servants (most of whom were white), excluded Indians altogether, and counted "all others" (meaning slaves) as three-fifths.

In addition, Article II, Section 9 permitted, until 1808, the importation and interstate trade of "such persons" as the States felt proper, with the payment of a tax. And Article IV, Section 2 provided that "no person held to service" who escaped into a free state would become free, but would be delivered back to the party claiming them.

Thus, for the sake of national unity, did the Constitution tacitly condone and attempt to resolve the question of slavery—without once mentioning the offensive word.

With Gen. Andrew Jackson at the Battle of New Orleans were·
Battalions of Negroes; one composed of business and profess·
men from New Orleans, the other including Creoles, Indians·
Negroes from St. Domingo.

Slavery as a factor in early political development.

The increase of anti-slavery sentiment—From its inception, slavery had been opposed by many of the colonists, most notably the Pennsylvania Quakers who organized the first anti-slavery groups in 1775. The majority of the Founding Fathers, though they may have owned slaves, were against the slave trade. Benjamin Franklin was a leader in the Society for Promoting the Abolition of Slavery, and Alexander Hamilton was active in the New York Manumission Society. Their persuasive moral arguments won over other colonial leaders to the cause, and by 1792 there were anti-slavery societies in every state from Massachusetts to Virginia. Joined by organizations of free blacks, and aided by the fact that slavery was unprofitable in the North, the abolitionists were instrumental in eliminating slavery in the northern states between 1775 and 1805.

The Northwest Ordinance—While the Constitution was still being written, the anti-slavery forces won the first round in the federal-power struggle with the Land Ordinance of 1787. In defining the political rights and liberties of people in the territories won from the British (from Ohio to Wisconsin), the last article of the Ordinance provided that "There shall be neither slavery nor involuntary servitude in such territory." Abolitionists felt sure that slavery was on the way out and would be ended by the twenty-year Constitutional deadline.

Slavery becomes a political institution—But the invention of the cotton gin in 1793 revived the cotton industry and increased the need for cheap labor that only black slaves seemed to be able to supply. Planters claimed that the prosperity of the South depended on slavery, politicians championed it, and churches tried to justify it on the grounds that the African-Americans were barbarians. The recaptur-

ing of fugitive slaves was made easier by the Fugitive Slave Laws of 1793; and states, cities, and communities began enacting various elaborate slave codes and "black laws" to control and restrict every phase of the slave's life. From defending and apoligizing for it the South turned to asserting that slavery was a positive good and "the cornerstone of our political edifice."

To the economic and cultural differences between the commercial North and the agricultural South was added their conflicting moral and political stance on slavery.

Slavery as a factor in the growth of the nation.

The Louisiana Purchase—The first large territorial acquisition of the new nation in 1803 was influenced by the institution of slavery both in the United States and in the French possession of Haiti. Led by the black Toussaint L'Ouveture, the Haitian slaves rebelled, and in a bloody war expelled the armies of Emperor Napoleon from the island. This manifestation of slave power made the United States fearful of an unrestricted importation by France of slaves into their Louisiana territory. At the same time Napoleon, who had invaded Europe, began to need money to finance his wars on the Continent. Abandoning his dreams of building an American empire on the lands of the Mississippi Valley, he accepted American proposals to purchase the Louisiana Territory.

The War of 1812—The country's first international conflict since its entry into the society of nations had little to do with slavery, nor did it add new lands to

ection of the painting "Mexican News—1848" by Alfred Jones shows egroes apparently uninterested. Most did not realize that the expansion of slave territories was a key issue in the war.

In Texas, slave cowboys broke in horses and herded cattle.

he nation. It did, however, encourage the growth of American nationalism, and also reaffirmed the fact hat Afro-Americans were an integral part of the nation's life and continued existence. It is estimated hat blacks comprised at least one-tenth of the crews of the victorious fleets of the Great Lakes; and all-lack regiments were formed in New York and Philadelphia. The most heroic service of Negroes vas performed at the Battle of New Orleans where laves and free men of color helped Gen. Andrew ackson's integrated forces achieve an overwhelming victory.

One of the settlements of the war was the rbitration of the lingering question of the slaves aptured by the British during the Revolutionary Var.

Expansion in the South and Midwest—With its ourse as an independent nation firmly established as result of the War of 1812, the United States entered a eriod of territorial growth and westward movement. In 1819, Florida was acquired from Spain after Gen. Andrew Jackson invaded the territory in 1817 to var against the Seminole Indians harboring fugitive

slaves. The two years of border warfare found blacks fighting both with the Americans and with the Indians. The treaties after the Seminole Wars relocated the Indians and their adopted black tribe members to Oklahoma and Kansas where some of their descendants may still be found. Florida was admitted to the Union as a slave state in 1845.

The matter of slavery first became an issue in the nation's growth in 1819 when Missouri applied for admission to the Union as a slave state. The resulting controversy was long and heated, and was only settled by balancing Missouri with the admission of Maine as a free state. This "Missouri Compromise" provided in part that thereafter slavery would be prohibited in the northern part of the Louisiana Purchase territory in order to keep slave states and free states in balance. It was hoped that the slavery difficulty was forever settled. "Forever" in this case was little more than twenty-five years.

Westward expansion—In the 1820s, American settlers, including slaveholders from the South, began entering the Southwest territories. Conflicts over government, land, and slavery soon broke out between the Mexicans and the Americans, and in 1836 the Texas colonists revolted and set up an independent republic. Texas became a depot for the importation of slaves from Havana, and its annexation to the United states was delayed until 1845 by Northern politicians who opposed the admission of another slave state.

The long-desired territories of New Mexico and California were won from Mexico in a war which began over a disputed boundary line of the new Republic of Texas. The Mexican War (1846-1848) was opposed by the North and favored by the South because Texas represented an additional slave state in the Union. When the outcome of this deliberately

By the mid-1800s the slavery question was being hotly debated in towns and villages across the nation, but the slaves themselves had little voice in the discussions.

provoked war became evident, David Wilmot, a Philadelphia Congressman, proposed in 1846 that slavery should be forever prohibited in all territory that might be acquired from Mexico. The proposal was defeated, but the "Wilmot Proviso" expressed a policy which two years later became the platform of the Free Soil Party, and later of the Republican Party.

In 1849, after the discovery of gold had brought thousands of American settlers into the area, California as an independent government applied for admission to the Union. The dream of a nation extending from the Atlantic Ocean to the Pacific Ocean was about to be realized.

But California's new population was made up of a majority from the North, including many free men of color. Their constitution excluded slavery, and their application for statehood was made as a free state. At the same time, Oregon, Minnesota and the newly acquired Mexican territories had submitted applications as non-slave states. Southerners were outraged at this threatened violation of the Missouri Compromise which would upset the balance of power in the Senate. The tense situation was aggravated by bitter Southern complaints that the North was disregarding the Fugitive Slave Law; and by indignant Northern demands that the District of Columbia abolish slavery and, indeed, all interstate slave traffic.

Slavery as a factor in testing the nation.

Though politically powerless, the black presence in America was the point upon which the future of the new nation seemed to be balanced. Anti-slavery sentiment was expressed in open interference with the arrest of fugitive slaves and assistance in their escape via the "Underground Railroad". Southern reaction reached the point of threats to reopen the slave trade in defiance of federal laws, and to seriously consider secession from the Union. Fights broke out in the hallowed chambers of the Senate. The debate was carried on in pamphlets and newspapers. The book "Uncle Tom's Cabin", an emotional anti-slavery appeal, became the nation's first best seller.

The Compromise of 1850—The violent feelings of both factions were temporarily soothed by the Compromise of 1850. Prepared by Henry Clay, the author of the Missouri Compromise thirty years previous, the new "Omnibus Bill" contained four essential provisions: (1) California was to be admitted as a free state (for the North); (2) but in the rest of the Mexican cession the people were to decide for themselves whether they would have slaves or not (for the South); (3) the slave trade—not slavery—was to be abolished in the Capitol (for the North, though not completely); (4) but a more severe Fugitive Slave Law was to be passed (for the South).

But the schism was too wide, the wounds too deep, the passions too inflamed, and the issues too complex to be settled by legislative compromise. Within four years the Compromise of 1850 was nullified by other legislation; and bloodshed decided the issue in Kansas and Nebraska. Within ten years the North and the South were poised for a civil war which would decide not only the fate of black Americans but the future of the nation as well.

CHRONOLOGY OF RELEVANT EVENTS

In many areas of the country Negroes, whether free or slaves, were harassed by pro-slavery whites.

784. Connecticut and Rhode Island abolish slavery.

786. Shay's Rebellion; Moses Sash, a black ex-soldier, is indicted the following year as captain and member of Shay's council in the revolt of Massachusetts farmers.

787. Northwest Ordinance excludes slavery from Northwest Territory.

788. Constitution ratified; protects property in slaves in three separate sections.

789. Benjamin Franklin appeals for funds to promote abolitionist activities.

790. America's first treaty (with the Creek Indians) contains a provision requiring the return of runaway slaves.

791. *Dec. 15:* Bill of Rights added to the Constitution to protect the people against the power of central government.

792. South Carolina suspends slave trade.

793. Invention of cottin gin spurs cotton industry and slavery.
Feb. 12: First Fugitive Slave Act passed.

1794. North Carolina prohibits slave trade; Congress prohibits exportation of slaves.

1796. Tennessee grants the vote to free Negroes.

1797. First recorded petition of free Negroes to bring more slaves out of bondage is refused by Congress.

1799. New York abolishes slavery.

1800. Slave revolt planned by Gabriel Prosser is betrayed.

1803. Louisiana Purchase opens up new lands for settlement.

1804. New Jersey abolishes slavery; Lewis and Clark, with slave York, start on their expedition.

1808. Federal law barring African slave trade goes into effect.

1812. *June 18:* War declared against England; blacks serve in American Army and Navy.

1818. First Seminole War involves many fugitive slaves who have joined Indians.

1819. Spain cedes Florida to U.S.; Indians and fugitive slaves face relocation; Missouri Compromise bars slavery in Louisiana Territory north of 36° 30'.

1827. *March 16:* First Negro newspaper, *Freedom's Journal,* published in New York City.
July 4: Slavery abolished in New York.

1831. William Lloyd Garrison begins publication of anti-slavery newspaper *Liberator.*

1833. American Anti-Slavery Society organized in Philadelphia by white and Negro abolitionists.

1836. Texas declares independence from Mexico; black participants in struggle disappointed in hope for free status.

1845. Texas annexed; statehood denied because of slave status.
March 3: Florida admitted to Union as slave state.
Dec. 29.: Texas admitted to Union as slave state after great controversy.

1846. Oregon Country claim is settled with Britain.
May 8: Mexican War begins at Palo Alto.
Aug. 8: David Wilmot introduces his Proviso in Congress.

1848. Women's rights and anti-slavery cause linked in first Women's Rights Convention.

1850. Clay Compromise attempts to reconcile slave-territory conflict between North and South.

1853. Gadsden Purchase adds new territory to U.S. southern border.

THE PEOPLE

Powerless and impoverished as a group, Afro-Americans as individuals, nevertheless, helped broaden the foundations of the new democracy, contributed to the wealth of the new capitalism, assisted in the conquests of the new nationalism, and enriched the culture of the new society.

Fighting for Liberty

Afro-Americans, having proven their capabilities, courage and determination in war, were found to be equally impelled in time of peace—their war for independence had not ended. Under repressive conditions and discouraging circumstances, leadership emerged.

Through the Church—Ministers and preachers were among the first spokesmen for the black members of a divided society attempting to define the directions and clarify the goals not reconciled by its Constitution.

During the war, Baptist churches had sprung up in the South. In 1779, George Liele founded a Baptist Church in Savannah, Georgia when the city was under British rule; he left the country soon after the war ended. When Andrew Bryan attempted to carry on his work under the Americans, members of the congregation were whipped and he was imprisoned.

Freed by sympathetic whites, Bryan was instrumental in spreading the Baptist movement to other cities in the North as well as the South.

Many slave ministers "in the practice of preaching of nights" ran away from their owners when this privilege was denied them. Reporting a runaway in 1793, one Baltimore slave owner said: "He was raised in a family of religious persons . . . and has lived with some of them . . . on terms of equality: the refusal to continue him on these terms gave him offense and he, therefore, absconded. He had been accustomed to instruct and exhort his fellow creatures of all colors in matters of religious duty."

Seeking greater privileges of worship in the North were Richard Allen and Alsalom Jones who had been pulled from their knees while praying in a white Philadelphia church. In the early decades of the 19th century, Allen founded the A.M.E. Church, and

Rev. George Leile, first Negro Baptist preacher, was ordained May 20, 1775.

James Varick, first bishop of the A.M.E. Zion Church established in 1801.

Catherine Ferguson, founder of the first Sunday School Movement in New York City in 1793.

John B. Russwurm, first Negro college graduate (1826) and founder of the first Negro newspaper, *Freedoms Journal*, in 1827.

Jones founded the African Episcopal Church in Philadelphia, while James Varick organized the A.M.E. Zion Church in New York, and Thomas Paul organized a Baptist congregation in Boston.

Through organized effort—These leaders did not confine their messages to spiritual matters. Allen started the first national movement for resettling free Negroes in Canada in 1830, and many others aided the escape of slaves via the newly organized Underground Railroad. The deeply religious Gabriel Prosser planned a Virginia rebellion in 1800; and the biblically inspired insurrectionists, Denmark Vessey and Nat Turner, plotted full-scale revolutions in 1822 and 1831.

Preferring relocation to revolution, outstanding ministers such as Alexander Crummell and Daniel Payne proposed Negro settlement in Africa. The versatile scholar Martin Delaney, and the prosperous businessman Paul Cuffe, also supported the idea. Businessman James Forten, however, violently opposed such notions, and lent his energies and monies to the abolition of slavery. The predominantly-white abolition movement started by the Quakers in the 1700s, was joined by many courageous and outspoken blacks by the mid 1800s: Robert Purvis, Samuel Cornish, James W.C. Pennington and Frederick Douglass were only a few who risked their lives and hard-earned reputations to goad the American conscience.

Contributing to the Economy

Given the chance, blacks were able to support themselves, own property, conduct businesses, and contribute to the growing prosperity of the nation. In the mid 1800s, blacks owned real estate valued in the hundred thousands of dollars in Philadelphia, Cincinnati, New York, Charleston, and New Orleans.

Individual cases of wealth among free blacks were numerous, and only a few can be mentioned. Henry Boyd of Cincinnati invented and manufactured a corded bed which was marketed throughout the Ohio and Mississippi valleys. Robert Gordon, also of Cincinnati, outwitted his white competitors in the coal business to corner the market and make a fortune in 1846. Solomon Humphries, a leading grocer in Macon, Georgia, accumulated property worth $20,000, including several slaves. John Jones, owner of one of Charleston's best hotels, amassed a fortune of more than $40,000. In Louisiana, Cyprean Ricard, Charles Rogues, and Marie Metoyer owned plantation estates complete with slaves. Thomy Lafon, the tycoon of New Orleans, was worth $500,000 at his death.

Samuel Cornish and John B. Russwurm published the first Negro newspaper in New York in 1827. In the next twenty years, several other cities in the North and West had black periodicals, most of which, like *The Frederick Douglass' Paper,* devoted their pages to educational articles and eloquent anti-slavery essays.

Enriching the Culture

Through education—In the effort to elevate themselves, blacks not only took advantage of the trend toward expanded education but contributed to it as well. Catherine Ferguson, born a slave in 1749, opened a School For The Poor in New York in 1793, and is credited with starting the Sunday School Movement. John Chavis, born free in 1763, attended several colleges and became a well-known preacher-teacher of whites and Negroes in North Carolina. He conducted his classes for Negroes in the evening, becoming one of the first to introduce night school and adult education. Today, a large park and housing project in Raleigh bear his name.

Through writing—With the opportunities for education open to free Negroes, black literature appeared. Most of the writing was journalistic, biographical or academic, but there were a few creative writers such as Jupiter Hammon, Phillis Wheatley, and later, Frances Harper. Although most of their writings were published after the mid-1800s, the urge to express themselves began in the post-Revolutionary period for such eloquent pamphleteers as David Walker, David Ruggles and Daniel Payne, to name only a few. A surprising number of escaped slaves were able to chronicle their experiences, which when published helped sway the country against slavery.

Through the Arts—In the arts, there was little time for, or interest in, music, theater, or painting except in the most affluent and aristocratic circles of white society. But on the plantations in the South, slaves were often asked to entertain the guests with song and dance; and in the fields black folk music—the roots of jazz, blues, and spirituals—was being born. In the visual arts the talented blacks usually became artisans in the various trades, and in New Orleans, created most of the fancy architectural iron work and grills for which the city became famous. A Rhode Island historian theorized that the famous colonial portrait artist, Gilbert Stuart, "derived his impression of drawing from witnessing Neptune Thurston, a slave who was employed in his master's cooper-shop."

Building the Nation

In the conquests of both land and peoples which forged the nation, blacks played their important supporting roles as soldiers, frontiersmen, and settlers. Their courage was often noted, but more often their names and race did not become part of our recorded history.

The War of 1812—The War of 1812 was ignited by such incidents as the British shelling of the United States naval vessel *Chesapeake* in 1807, which killed and wounded many Americans. Four prisoners were seized by the British and charged with desertion from the British Navy, but only one was convicted. The three who were able to prove their innocence were three black sailors, John Strackan, Daniel Martin, and William Ware.

In one naval battle of the war, Nathaniel Shaler, an American officer, noted:

"The name of one of my poor fellows who was killed ought to be registered in the book of fame, and remembered with reverence as long as bravery is considered a virtue. He was a black man, by the name of John Johnson. A twenty-four-pound shot struck him in the hip, and took away all the lower part of his body. In this state, the poor brave fellow lay on the deck, and several times exclaimed to his shipmates, 'Fire away, my boys: no haul a color down.' The other was also a black man, by the name of John Davis, and was struck in much the same way. He fell near me, and several times requested to be thrown overboard, saying he was only in the way of the others. When America has such tars, she has little to fear from the tyrants of the ocean."

Before the Battle of New Orleans on January 8, 1815, General Andrew Jackson referred to his Negro troop as "adopted children", and appealed to them to "rally around the standard of the eagle, to defend all which is dear in existence." Over four hundred volunteered on the promise of equal treatment and equal pay; and during the ferocious fighting, the British Gen. Pakenham was believed by Jackson to have been killed by "a free man of color, who was a famous rifle shot."

The Southeast—Florida was a refuge for runaway slaves before it was sold by Spain, a fact which angered the American slave owners. In one incident, a fort occupied by three hundred Seminoles and blacks, and under the command of the Negro, Garcia, was blown up, killing almost all its occupants. After the sale of Florida in 1819, three Seminole Wars were fought to subdue and expel the Indians and their Negro allies. During these wars, blacks fought on both sides; Gopher John was one of many black scouts and interpreters used by the American forces. Negro Abraham was one of the best known leaders and interpreters for the Seminoles. Louis Pacheco, slave hired by the Americans, became a double agent and led a U.S. troop into the ambush known as "Dades Massacre."

The Central Region—The Northwest Territories ceded to the U.S. in 1783, as free states were the haven for many escaped slaves as well as free Negroes who ttled there. De Sable, the Haitian trapper, esta-ished a trading post in Peoria, Illinois; explored ound the Great Lakes; and became Chicago's first ttler in 1774. One of the first blacks in the Cleveland ea was an escaped slave, Ben, who hid out in the oods near Brecksville in 1809. George Peake, a free egro and former soldier of the British Army, settled ear Lakewood, Ohio that year; he later won promi-ence as the inventor of a new type of hand mill. Well nown to Cleveland in 1831 was John Manville, a ioneer preacher, engineer, sailing master, canal-oat captain, educator and abolitionist.

In 1833, a party of 385 black men, women and hildren came into Mercer County, Ohio, to claim nd willed to them by their wealthy master. Cheated ut of the land, they scattered throughout Ohio and diana. Some may have joined the Roberts family ho earlier had settled in Hamilton County, Indi-a. Two black missionaries, John Marrant of New ork and John Stewart of Virginia, traveled the idwest preaching to the Indians.

The vast regions of the Louisiana Territory, rchased from France in 1803, were explored by ewis and Clark whose expedition included the ack slave, York. On the two and one-half year trek the Columbia River and back, York served as ide, hunter, interpreter, and other roles beyond his atus as slave. Helping to open up the West in later ears were many blacks seeking adventure and new ontiers of freedom. The mountain man James eckwourth blazed one of the most traveled trails to alifornia. Hiram Young, a Negro blacksmith, pros-ered in Independence, Missouri, building the wag-s that lumbered over the western trails. Three acks—Oscar Crosby, Green Flake, and Hark Lay—ere with the party that preceeded the first Mormon ioneers to the valley of the Great Salt Lake in 1847. heir names are inscribed on a monument in Salt ake City.

he Southwest—Accompanying many of the first ttlers in Texas were slaves, some of whom escaped join the Indians, and others who protected their wners with their very lives. A slave of Jim Bowie, ventor of the famous throwing knife, helped fight ff a Comanche attack in 1831. During the battle he ashed to a spring to bring back water for the settlers. ob Anderson and a teenage slave named Smith rvived Indian attacks on the ranches of their separ-e masters. With a butcher knife in one hand and a istol in the other, Smith killed one Indian, ounded another, and drove the third back into the ilderness. In the fight for independence preceeding s annexation, Texas utilized black soldiers from the onflict's first battle at the Alamo to the final battle at n Jacinto. Hendrick Arnold, a free black, served as scout for three American regiments. Greenburg

Logan, another free black, was awarded Texas citiz-enship and land for the disabling wounds he received in the many battles he fought for Texas independence.

Even after economics and Southern sentiment, brought Texas into the Union as a slave state, many blacks continued to contribute to its development. The Aaron Ashworth family, arriving in Texas in 1833, were the owners of a large cattle ranch by 1850. Isham Hicks, another free black, supervised the construction of the First Methodist Church in Comanche County, and was later killed in an Indian raid.

The West Coast Regions—Africans had participated in the Spanish explorations of the Pacific Coast in the 1500's, and some had served in California with the Mexicans in the 1700's, settling in the areas now known as Los Angeles, Santa Barbara, and San Francisco. Marcus Lopeus, member of an expedition headed by Capt. Gray, was the first known African to arrive in the Northwest in 1788; he was later killed by Indians. With American interest in the region increa-sing in the 1800's, many blacks accompanied the exploring and hunting parties into the area. In 1827, Peter Ranne crossed the San Bernadino Mountains with the explorer Jededia Smith and reached the California mission of San Gabriel.

Alexander Leidesdorf, a wealthy New Orleanian, sailed his 160-ton schooner to San Francisco in 1841 and remained there to become one of its leading citizens. George William Bush, one of the leading pioneers of Oregon and Washington, led his wife, five children and several white couples from the Mexican border to the Columbia River in 1844, to become the first American settlers north of the river. The trail blazer, James Beckwourth, first reached California in 1844, followed shortly thereafter by hundreds of settlers and their slaves. Eighteen-year-old Jacob Dodson, a free black, came to California with the Fremont expedition, and later fought along-side Fremont and Kit Carson in California's war for independence.

After the territory came under U.S. control and gold was discovered in 1848, prospecting slavehold-ers flooded into California. Some slaves such as Alvin Coffey, Daniel Rogers, and Saunders Jackson earned their freedom working in the gold fields. Coffey bought his and his family's freedom for $7,000 and became a respected farmer in Red Bluff. Rogers was cheated out of his liberty by his master, but fair-minded whites replaced the money. Jackson, a slave of Fremont, mined $1,700 which he exchanged for his liberty. Thousands of free and slave blacks amassed considerable wealth, and by 1850 California was one of America's richest Negro communities.

Benjamin Banneker   (1731-1806)

"SABLE GENIUS"

The Afro-American making the greatest variety of contributions to the life and culture of the new nation was Benjamin Banneker, an intellectual giant who achieved in the fields of science, mathematics, astronomy, agriculture and writing.

Born near Baltimore, Maryland, Banneker attended an integrated school, and early developed an interest in science and mathematics as well as an aptitude in mechanics. In 1761, with very simple tools and a borrowed watch he constructed from wood a clock that struck the hours and kept good time, "the first clock of which every portion was made in America."

His mechanical genius attracted the attention of George Ellicot, the owner of a local flour mill, who became a life-long friend of Banneker. Through his library, Ellicot encouraged Banneker's interest in science, and in a short time Banneker had earned a reputation among the local farmers as a source for all kinds of information and a solver of all types of problems. In 1789 he had become so proficient in astronomy that he was able to predict a solar eclipse.

In 1791 he began publishing an almanac in which, from time to time, he included various provocativ[e] essays. In addition to daily weather and astronomica[l] information, Banneker's writings included a treatis[e] on bees, a mathematical study of the 17-year locust, [a] remarkably complete "plan for peace," and article[s] proving the ability of blacks to achieve. He sen[t] Secretary of State Thomas Jefferson a copy of his firs[t] almanac along with a letter in which he proteste[d] Jefferson's growing prejudice against the Negro[.] Jefferson wrote a complimentary reply and for[-] warded the almanac to the Academy of Science i[n] Paris, but he never really changed his attitude.

Banneker's most distinguished hour was h[is] appointment to the commission assisting th[e] Frenchman Pierre Charles L'Enfant in laying out th[e] new capitol city of Washington, D.C. The story [is] told that when the temperamental L'Enfant becam[e] angered and returned to France with all of h[is] drawings, Ellicot, the chief surveyor, and Banneke[r] were able to reproduce them from memory. Th[e] present District of Columbia is based on the L'Enfa[nt] plans which were completed with the assistance o[f] the "sable genius", Benjamin Banneker.

Lavinia Dobler and Edgar Toppin, *Pioneers and Patriots* (New York: Double[day] and Co., 1965).

Richard Allen   (1760-1831)

SPOKESMAN

The opposition to the anti-slavery efforts of the Quakers and other groups after the war caused many Negroes to question the wisdom of their continued loyalty to the new nation.

However, Richard Allen, founder of the African Methodist Episcopal Church, spoke for the vast majority of blacks when he said, "We were stolen from our mother country, and brought here. We have tilled the ground and made fortunes for thousands . . . This land which we have watered with our tears and our blood, is now our mother country."

Allen, born a slave in Pennsylvania during the Revolutionary era, had never been confused about his loyalties. He was sold to a planter in Dover, Delaware and, converted to Methodism at 17, became such a persuasive preacher that he converted his master who agreed to sell him his liberty. During the war, Allen made enough money as a wood cutter and wagoner to purchase freedom for himself and his brother in 1783. The first years of Allen's freedom were spent in traveling with a Methodist minister, occasionally being allowed to preach to the mixed congregations.

After preaching at Philadelphia's St. George Methodist Episcopal Church in 1786, his black following increased and the churches began segregating the congregations, and even discouraging black attendance. In protest, one Sunday in 1787, Allen and his followers walked out, and soon after founded the Bethel African Methodist Episcopal Church, which still occupies its original site a few blocks from Independence Hall.

As first bishop of the A.M.E. Church, Allen not only ministered to the spiritual needs of the black community but worked militantly for their education and advancement. When a yellow fever epidemic struck Philadelphia in 1793, Allen organized a massive relief effort. During the War of 1812, when the city was threatened by the British, he helped raise 2,500 Negro troops for its defense. In 1817 his Bethel Church was the center of protest against the newly formed American Colonization Society whose program was to deport blacks from what Allen had long since decided was their "mother country".

Russell Adams, *Great Negroes Past and Present* (Chicago: Afro-Am Publ. Co., 1969). Carter Woodson and Charles Wesley, *Negro Makers of History* (Washington, D.C.: Associated Publishers, 1958).

Paul Cuffe   (1759-1817)

FREEDOM-SEEKING BUSINESSMAN

A silhouette is the only known portrait of Cuffe.

During the post-Revolutionary period, many black folk began to feel that no matter what service they rendered to their country they would not be allowed the complete enjoyment of "life, liberty and the pursuit of happiness." One of the most outstanding Negroes who sought an answer to this despair through economic independence and group self-respect was Paul Cuffe. Born free, and self educated, he was the owner of a fleet of ships at 35, but died believing the frontiers of freedom for Negroes would only be found in Africa.

Cuffe, son of an African father and Indian mother, and a native of Massachusetts, became interested in shipping when he joined a whaling crew at the age of sixteen. Throughout the Revolutionary War he worked as a seaman, and was once captured and imprisoned by the British for three months. When he was twenty, he and his brother built their first ship, an open boat for trading with the people of Connecticut. Over the next twenty-five years he acquired more and larger ships, the largest being the 268-ton *Alpha* with a crew of nine. It was on one of his trading trips that he first got the idea of establishing a colony of Afro-Americans in Africa which could be supported by trade between it and the mother country.

Although he was a prosperous businessman, Cuffe was an early champion of equal rights and the abolition of slavery. He took the name of Cuffe when he was seventeen because his original name, Slocum, was the name of his father's former master. During the Revolutionary War, in 1780, he and his brother sued for the right to vote because they were the taxpayers. After his marriage in 1783, he built a school and hired a teacher when he found there were no facilities for Negroes in the area. As time passed he became more and more convinced that colonization in Africa was the answer to the plight of free Afro-Americans.

In the face of many obstacles, Cuffe made two attempts to establish a colony in British-owned Sierra Leone, Africa—in 1811 and in 1815—paying for the second trip with $4,000 of his own money. Both attempts failed to gain the support of many Afro-Americans, as did later arguments of the American Colonization Society. Cuffe died a wealthy but frustrated man.

Russell Adams, *Great Negroes Past and Present* (Chicago: Afro-Am Publishing Co., 1969). Esther Douty, *Forten the Sailmaker* (New York: Rand McNally & Co., 1968). William C. Nell, *Colored Patriots of the American Revolution* (Boston: Robert F. Wallcutt, 1855).

James Forten (1766-1842)

ABOLITIONIST BUSINESSMAN

The appeal of liberty and independence during the war was so powerful as to impress itself upon the minds of even those who could not conceive of its political application. At the age of fourteen, James Forten, the son of free Philadelphia Negroes, persuaded his mother to let him sign on as powder boy aboard the American privateer *Royal Louis*. When he was captured by the British and offered a chance to go to England, Forten answered, "I am here a prisoner for the liberties of my country. I never, never, shall prove a traitor to her interest."

James was imprisoned for seven months before being freed near the end of the war. His early love of liberty—and distaste for restriction—was later directed toward the liberation of his fellow Afro-Americans. His adolescent patriotism became the basis for his later opposition to proposals for returning Negroes to Africa.

In 1787, Forten went to work in a Philadelphia sailmaking shop, and at twenty-two was made foreman over forty workers, half of whom were white. He eventually became owner of the business and, partly due to a sailmaking device he invented, he developed one of the most prosperous shops in the city. As a respected and influential figure, he accrued a fortune of over $100,000, much of which he spent in the fight to abolish slavery.

During the War of 1812, Forten assisted in organizing blacks for the defense of Philadelphia; at the same time he was busily writing letters of protest against proposed legislation restricting the Negroes of the city. His powerful writings, published in a pamphlet called "A Series of Letters by A Man of Color" helped defeat the (Negro) Registration bill of 1813.

Forten's most painful fight was against his friend, Paul Cuffe, and the American Colonization Society who both advocated the resettlement of Negroes in Liberia. But despite strong bonds of friendship, Forten upheld his early vow never to betray what he felt was the interest of his country.

Esther Douty, *Forten the Sailmaker* (New York: Rand McNally, 1968).

James Derham   (1762- ?)   PHYSICIAN

Blacks, as slaves and as free men, contributed to the meager medical knowledge of the post-Revolutionary period. Many slaves brought with them from Africa a knowledge of herbs, drugs and potions as well as "vodoo" practices which effected remarkable cures. As barbers having the tools for cutting and bleeding, free blacks frequently also served as physicians. James Derham, born into slavery, learned his art while serving as assistant to his several physician masters.

Derham was originally owned by Dr. John Kearley, Jr. of Philadelphia, who taught him to read and write. During the Revolutionary War, Derham was acquired by Dr. George West, a surgeon in the Sixteenth British Regiment, and increased his medical knowledge by assisting in the treatment of wounded soldiers. When the British troops left the country in 1783, Derham was sold to Dr. Robert Dove of New Orleans, who was so impressed by the ability of his new assistant that within a few years he allowed Derham to purchase his freedom on very liberal terms.

With the help of Dr. Dove, Derham set up his own office, and soon built up a large practice among Negroes and whites. By 1788 he was one of the top physicians in New Orleans. Later that same year, his fame spread even farther when he met Dr. Benjamin Rush, an eminent surgeon and graduate of the University of Edinburgh. Dr. Rush had served as the surgeon-general in the Continental Army during the war, and was a professor at the Philadelphia Medical School.

Meeting Dr. Derham in Philadelphia where he had gone to be baptized in the Episcopal Church, Dr. Rush later wrote of the skilled black physician: "I have conversed with him upon most of the acute and epidemic disease of the country where he lives (Louisiana) and was pleased to find him perfectly acquainted with the modern simple mode of practice in those diseases. I expected to have suggested some new medicines to him; but he suggested many more to me."

Wilhelmena Robinson, *Historical Negro Biographies* (New York: Publishers Co., 1967). Woodson and Wesley, *Negro Makers of History* (Washington, D.C., Associated Publishers, Inc., 1958).

(Not a portrait)

Joshua Johnston   (c. 1770-1830)

ARTIST

"Gentleman of the Shure Family" painted about 1810.

It was not until after the Revolutionary War that the skills of talented African slaves could be diverted from the labors of carpentry, metal working and similar crafts to the decorative and fine arts of interior and exterior ornament, engraving, carving, and painting. Increased prosperity, education, and good taste promoted a desire for aesthetic appeal, and many blacks were given the chance to move up from artisans to artists.

Joshua Johnston was the first American artist of African descent to attain status and recognition as a portrait painter. Not much is known about his early life, but indications are that, whether born free or slave, he was a native American and was probably raised in the area of Baltimore, Maryland. He may have begun his art career as a ship or house painter. Similarities between his work and that of Charles Peale Polk lead to the belief that he was a student of this well-known artist.

A free man by his early twenties, he apparently acquired a better-than-average education and enough polish and talent to become acceptable in white society by 1796. The Baltimore Official Directories from 1796 to 1824 list Johnston as a "Free Householder of Colour" with his occupation as "portrait painter."

Twenty-five portraits are now definitely attributed to Johnston, and about twenty-five more reveal unmistakable characteristics of his work. Most of the paintings are of leading Baltimoreans or their families. It is obvious that he was a popular and fashionable artist of the early 1800s. In his lifetime, Johnston's paintings were treasured works exhibited only in the homes of his sitters. Today his paintings are in the National Gallery of Art in Washington, D.C., the Maryland Historical Society, and the Baltimore Museum of Art.

Alain Locke, *The Negro In Art* (Chicago: Afro-Am Press, 1969). Bearden, and Henderson, *Six Black Masters of American Art* (New York: Doubleday & Co., 1972).

(Not a portrait)

George Bonga   (1802- ?)

MINNESOTA TRADER

One year before the eastern part of Minnesota came into U.S. possession from the defeated British, Jean and Marie Bonga (or Bonza) were brought into the territory as the slaves of Capt. Daniel Robertson, the British commander of the outpost at Michilimackinac. One of the Bonga children, Pierre, grew up to be a fur trader in the employ of the North West Company in Detroit. Pierre's son, George, also entered the fur trading business and lived to become "a thorough gentleman in both feeling and deportment . . . a man of wealth and consequence."

Born west of Duluth near the mouth of the St. Louis River, George became a *voyaguer* for John Jacob Astor's American Fur Company, traveling the Great Lakes and tributary rivers in a frail birch bark canoe collecting pelts. Bonga was a powerful man, six feet tall, weighing over 200 pounds with "sinews and cords in his limbs like a horse." He was said to have packed 700 pounds on his back in a quarter mile portage around the rapids of the St. Louis River. He was also noted for his political knowledge and intelligence, able to speak English, French, and the Chippewa tongue.

When Gov. Cass charted the area of Lake Superior in 1820, he asked Bonga to act as interpreter with the Ojibway Indians. Bonga's services were also used at the signing of the Chippewa Treaty and the establishing of the Methodist Episcopal Church for Indians in 1837; and during the 1860s for the Indian agent, Joel Bassett.

Bonga was a licensed Indian trader from about 1830 to 1868, and like his father, married a Chippewa Indian. As in other sections of the country, the explorers and the traders became the first settlers, and by 1897, an estimated one hundred descendents of the Bonga's had helped settle the state of Minnesota.

George Reasons, *They Had A Dream*, Vol. II (Los Angeles: L.A. Times Syndicate, 1970). William Katz, *Eyewitness: The Negro in American History* (New York: Pitman, 1967).

York

WITH LEWIS AND CLARK

One of the most famous explorations in American history is the 1804-1806 expedition led by Meriwether Lewis and William Clark which explored the Louisiana Territory. Aiding the success of the expedition was Clark's slave, York. An excellent swimmer, hunter and fisherman, York served as guide, scout and boatman, but his greatest skill proved to be his ability to win friends among the Indians encountered on the long and dangerous trip.

Clark's journals mention York many times, and one entry notes: ". . . The three great Chiefs and many others came to see us today . . . much astonished at my black Servent, who did not lose the opportunity of (displaying) his powers . . ." The following day, ". . . all flocked around him & examined him from top to toe, he carried on the joke and made himself more turribal than we wished him to doe." When York danced with the Indians one New Year's Day it "amused the Crowd verry much, and somewhat astonished them, that so large a man should be active . . ." Later in the journey, York tired of his entertainer role, and when one skeptical chief wet his finger to see if the black would rub off, York pulled his knife and glared fiercely at him.

York helped provide food by hunting buffalo, bear, deer and other game, as well as gathering nuts, berries "wild Creases and Tung grass." On one occasion a sudden thunderstorm caused a flash flood to trap Clark and an Indian with her baby in a torrent of swirling water. York helped rescue the three and, Clark recalled, "was greatly agitated for our welfar."

After two and a half years of incredible hardships the expedition reached the Pacific Ocean at the mouth of the Columbia River and made the return trip to St. Louis. York was given his freedom and, while one report has him dying of cholera years later, another says he rejoined the Indians and lived in the territory he helped explore.

Phillip Drotning, *Black Heroes In Our History* (New York: Washington Square Press, 1970).

James Beckwourth (1798-1867)

MOUNTAIN MAN

The settlement of the vast frontier lands west of the Mississippi River was spearheaded by the hardy men who dared the dangers of the wilderness and hostile Indians for riches or just for mere adventure. Among these trappers, traders and mountain men were such legendary figures as Kit Carson, Daniel Boone, Jim Bowie—and the mulatto Jim Beckwourth.

Son of a Revolutionary War officer and his black slave, Beckwourth was born in Virginia but migrated with his family to Missouri. He apprenticed as a blacksmith, at eighteen ran away, and in 1823 joined General Ashley's Rocky Mountain Fur Company. Leaving the expedition in 1825, he lived among the Blackfoot and Crow Indians where he became a warrior and chief who took part in their tribal battles. He lived with the Crow for six years, then left to roam the nation from Florida to Mexico, and west to California, establishing a fabulous reputation as explorer, woodsman, trapper, hunter, guide, scout, interpreter and fighter.

He became a scout for "the pathfinder", Gen. John C. Fremont; helped Kit Carson carry the news to Washington of the discovery of gold in California and discovered a mountain pass through the High Sierras which bears his name. The trail he laid out to California became the route of the Western Pacific Railroad, fostering the birth of Reno, Nevada. In 1844, he became a messenger for Gen. Kearny and later took part in the Mexican War. He joined the Colorado goldrush of 1859, and after a brief spell of ranching on the Feather River in California, fought in the Cheyenne War of 1864.

Beckwourth's own account of his life is so adventure-filled that many historians refuse to accept it as truth. One of his more believable stories told how his expert marksmanship saved General Ashley's life when he was charged by a wounded buffalo. As the animal's horns neared the helpless General, Jim, some distance away, raised his rifle and fired. The ball struck just behind the buffalo's shoulders, "instantly dropping him dead."

It was ironic but somehow fitting that James Beckwourth died while on a mission of peace with the Crow Indians in behalf of the U.S. government.

J.P. Beckwourth, *The Life and Adventures of James P. Beckwourth* (New York: D Voto, 1931).

Negro Abraham   WITH THE FLORIDA INDIANS

The purchase of Florida from Spain in 1819 came about as the indirect result of the fraternity which existed between red men and black men. Each year, hundreds of slaves valued by their owners at about $2,000 each, ran away from plantations in the Georgia territory and joined the Indians of Florida. On the excuse of punishing Indian marauders and hunting runaway slaves, the U.S. army invaded the Indian villages in the Spanish territories in 1817, and incited the First Seminole War. In treaties relocating the Creeks and Seminoles from Florida to Oklahoma and Kansas after the war, reference is made to "their faithful interpreter, Abraham."

Negro Abraham (Black Abraham) was a fugitive slave adopted by the Seminole Indians. Born in Pensacola, Florida, in the early 1800s, he escaped and sought shelter with the Seminoles in 1826. He learned the language and customs, and became known as "prophet", "principal counselor of his master, Chief Micanopy," and "high chancellor and keeper of the king's conscience." An American officer described him as having "the crouch and spring of a panther."

Although uneducated, he was a persuasive and eloquent speaker; "a perfect Talleyrand of the Savage Court of Florida," said one writer. As one of the spokesmen and interpreters for the Seminole nation, he at first opposed their relocation, not only because it was an injustice to the Indians but because he feared that, in traveling across the Southern states, many of the Negroes would be recaptured by the slave hunters.

He also opposed mingling the Seminoles with the Creeks because the latter were known to enslave Negroes; and in the Fort Dade Treaty of 1837, demanded a guarantee against domination by the Creeks. In 1838, he finally helped convince the tribes to accept the U.S. demands for the sake of the women and children. Negotiating to secure the best terms possible, he agreed to investigate the proposed site in Oklahoma, and refused to the move until he was assured of everybody's freedom.

Wilhelmena Robinson, *Historical Negro Biographies* (New York: Publishers Co., 1967). Benjamin Brawley, *A Social History of the American Negro* (New York: Collier Books, 1970).

Manuel Camero (1751- ?)

A FOUNDER OF LOS ANGELES

Of the twelve men, nine were Negro, mulatto, mestizo or Indian; only two were Spaniards. The women and children were of mixed ancestry—Spanish, Indian, and Negro. Manuel Camero was a mulatto.

The group had been recruited by an emissary of Gov. Felipe de Neve who promised each settler farm animals, farming tools and a musket. Manuel and his wife Maria left their home in Sonora, Mexico to join the group, putting themselves in bondage for ten years to pay for the trip. He was to be paid $116 a year in clothing and supplies for the first two years, and $60 annually for the next three.

Each family was assigned a plot of land on the perimeter of the planned pueblo, whose center was to be a plaza 200 feet by 300 feet with its eastern side reserved for public buildings. By the end of 1784, the settlers had completed their homes and most of the public buildings, and had begun work on a chapel. Camero built his adobe home on land given him by a formal Spanish grant in 1786.

In 1788, the first elections were held, and in the following year's election Emanuel Camero and one Felipe Garcia were elected as the pueblo's first *regidores*, or town councilmen. By 1790, Los Angeles had 139 residents, a town hall, a barracks, a guardhouse and graneries, and was one of California's most productive settlements.

George Reasons, *They Had A Dream*, Vol. I (Los Angeles: L.A. Times Syndicate, 1969).

Before the English colonies on the Atlantic coast became involved in the Revolutionary War, the Spaniards had already established Franciscan missions along the California coast. To settle the land, Spain encouraged people from her colonies in Mexico to move north. In 1781, a racially mixed group of twelve families arrived in southern California and founded "El Puelblo de Nuestra Senora la Reina de Los Angeles de Prociuncula." This small settlement with the long name later became the large city with the shorter name, "Los Angeles".

Allen B. Light

SOLDIER FOR CALIFORNIA

Between independence from Spain in 1822 and admission into the union in 1850, California waged a little-known fight for independence while under Mexican rule. Juan Bautista Alvarado, a revolutionary challenging the power of Mexico in California, in 1836 organized a small army, and for two dollars a day hired a group of mercenaries to supplement his forces. With about seventy-five men he marched on San Fernando and captured it without firing a shot. One of the mercenaries was the black hunter Allen B. Light.

Though belonging to Mexico at the time, California was often invaded by British and American ships bringing Indians and trappers on hunting forays. Light was a sailor on the *Pilgrim,* a trading vessel from Boston. On one of the trips to the California waters in the early 1830s he jumped ship and joined other frontiersmen who journeyed up and down the coast from Monterey to San Diego. Traveling in frail canoes or whaleboats, Light and his companions faced dangers from the elements and the wild animals as well as from the Indians who would kill hunters to get their pelts. On one occasion the hunters turned back an attack of twenty-six warriors in thirteen canoes.

In contrast to his name, Light was very dark and was sometimes called "Black Steward." He was considered to be "intelligent, well behaved, mannerly and a good hunter." However, one day in 1835 while tracking a wounded deer, he got careless and was almost killed by a grizzly bear. A powerful man, Light killed the bear with his knife, but not before his arm was rendered useless by the bear's jaws.

For his stint as a mercenary soldier, Light was paid $5. He returned to Santa Barbara and to his hunting, and in 1841 was given the very tame job of preventing illegal hunting in coastal waters.

George Reasons, *They Had A Dream,* Vol. III (Los Angeles: L.A. Times Syndicate, 1971).

George Washington   (1817-1905)

FOUNDER OF CENTRALIA

As has been shown many times by African Americans, taking the name of a famous white man does little to ease the life of a black man. Born in Virginia, the same state as his namesake, black George Washington had to cross the entire country before being able to enjoy the respect and dignity due him.

Washington, a mulatto, was raised by the Cochrans, a white family who took him with them to Ohio and later to Missouri where, as a young man, he became owner of a saw mill. When a white man refused to pay for a load of lumber, Washington found out that he had no right to sue for payment. Moving to Illinois, Washington had a similar experience when he applied for a license to make whiskey.

In 1850, he and his foster parents moved to Oregon City, Washington, where he built a home and took a job as lumberjack at nine dollars a month to support the Cochrans. He staked out a claim of 640 acres at the fork of the Skookumchuck and Chehalis Rivers in Washington, fenced it in and planted twelve acres of oats. Then he was told about the law which prohibited Negroes from settling on state land. Washington quickly had his foster father register the claim in his name, and four years later bought it from him for $3,000.

For a time the two men raised cattle and sheep, and operated an inn and a ferry. In 1872, when the Northern Pacific Railroad purchased a right-of-way across his land, Washington laid out a townsite on his property, including park land, a cemetery and choice lots for churches. He originally called it Centerville but later changed it to Centralia.

Selling lots for five dollars, and offering free moving services, he and Centralia were soon prospering. When depression hit the town in 1893, the paternalistic Washington bought food and loaned large sums of money to keep the community going. When he died, a day of mourning was proclaimed and his funeral was the biggest in the city's history.

George Reasons, *They Had A Dream*, Vol. I (Los Angeles: L.A. Times Syndicate, 1969). Wilhelmena Robinson, *Historical Negro Biographies* (New York, Publishers Co., 1967).